Open

Jessie MOSS

A LIBERATING GUIDE TO SHED OLD
STORIES AND BECOME SELF-LED

CRAFT THE AWARE HEART

CHOOSE TO BE FREE

DISCLAIMER

This book came through me to you as a guide to empowerment from the inside out. It is not intended to be a replacement for professional help but a resource for guidance as you take the path to discover more about yourself. While you may find this book helpful and transformative I do encourage incorporating a team of support around you and to seek help from other professionals. Always take what resonates with you and leave behind what doesn't along your healing journey.

Jessie MOSS

Copyright © 2022 by Jessie Moss

All rights reserved. No part of this book may be reproduced in any manner whatsoever without written permission except in the case of brief quotations embodied in critical articles and reviews.

First Printing, 2022

Cover Design: Aleisha Henslee - pepdigital.com.au
Family Portrait Drawing: My talented son - Kayn Fitzgerald
Cover Illustration of the snake I have tattooed on my chest: Cherish @cherish.tattoos
Author Photo on the back cover: Anna Gilbert - annagilbert.com.au
Editing Love and a big thank you to Soul Scribe Sally Jane Friday - sallyjanefriday.com

WEBSITE

www.jessiemoss.com

> YOU WON'T EXPERIENCE YOUR HIGHEST TRUTH BY DOING NOTHING - YOU HAVE TO BE CURIOUS AND WILLING TO SHOW UP FOR IT.
> *-JESSIE MOSS*

DEDICATION

THIS BOOK IS DEDICATED TO THE ONES I CHOSE TO WOUND ME THE MOST. THANK YOU FOR GIVING ME THE GIFT OF BEING ABLE TO SEE, FEEL, KNOW, ACCESS, AND EMBODY THE HIGHEST TRUTH AND AUTHENTIC LIGHT WITHIN MYSELF.

YOU SHOWED ME THAT I GET TO WRITE A NEW BEGINNING

THAT I BELONG UNAPOLOGETICALLY AS I AM

THAT I WILL ALWAYS RISE.

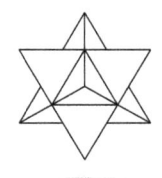

CONTENTS

1. Dear Truth Seeker — 1
2. Decide — 4
3. Surrender the story — 11
4. Invitation to heal — 32
5. Call your power back — 48
6. Expanded heart — 66
7. Truth is calling — 88
8. Inner world awakening — 114
9. Gratitude in oneness — 136

GRATITUDE AND ACKNOWLEDGMENT TO MY SONS,

For being the why to the choice I made to wake up and do better every day, for being patient while I cultivated the strength and heart needed for awakening, and for smiling with infinite love while we moved through difficult times of making hard choices together. Thank you for choosing me to guide you.

To Kayn, thank you for seeing so many versions of me and loving every single one of them along the way so unconditionally. You teach me the depth of love daily. Staying open and unconditional in love is your superpower. I am so proud of the wise, caring man you are becoming.

To Noah, thank you for keeping me on my toes and expanding me daily. Your untameable and curious nature reminds me to live deeper and laugh more often. Always be you. The world is lucky to have the unique gift of your presence. Keep aiming for the stars.

Dear Truth Seeker

> *THE POINT OF POWER IS ALWAYS IN THE PRESENT MOMENT.*
> *- LOUISE L HAY*

I love opening a book in wonder about what kind of a ride it has in store for me. This book was written with the same intention, of taking you on a journey to the depths of you. May you land with ease into the most exquisite alignment, right at the core of stirring heartfelt awakenings. As you settle in, gift yourself loving presence and space on this journey. Allow a truthful willingness to guide you through any realisations you meet along the way, knowing I will be right here with you, reminding you to choose yourself, to let things move through you, and to trust something bigger than life itself has your back through the entire process.

My name is Jessie Moss. I delve heart first into life's learnings and deep self-work to connect with insights and realisations through my own experiences of awakening. I then choose to share the wisdom and lessons as a facilitator of awakening and change, creating that key shift for others in a time of transition. In showing up as authentic as I can in each moment, my intention is to reflect truth in the world. In this truth I align with those who need that same resonance of truth—every time, at exactly the right time. It's a beautiful process to be part of.

As I support change and growth in humanity, I am very blessed to witness alignment to awakening all around me.

I have reached a point on my road to healing and thriving from trauma, abuse, and domestic violence to a place where I have cleared space in and all around me to be in service. This space has asked me to let go of my victim mentality over and over again. It has asked me to view my wounds as gifts, my addictions as suppression, and to be compassionate toward my actions with an understanding that it was the only way I knew how to cope at the time. The new perspective from a clearer space asked me to let go of the deeply embedded patterns of suffering and the dysfunctional way of surviving I was so accustomed to. And most importantly, it asked me to be forgiving of my own mistakes.

Sharing my own journey helps others align to their true authentic self—a self that experiences passion, play and ease while remaining true to their values. A self that is free of the suffering, one who feels worthy, seen and able to deservingly create their desired future. If your aligned self is calling for such liberation through understanding and openness, then I am so excited and honoured that you are here. Let's not wait any longer to get stuck in, freedom awaits…

2

Decide

> *I AM NOT WHAT HAPPENED TO ME,*
> *I AM WHAT I CHOOSE TO BECOME.*
> -CARL JUNG

ENTERING A CHAPTER OF DECISION

A journey to the self has begun.

By simply picking up this book you have made the decision to rewrite a brand-new story for yourself.

Before we begin, I want to clearly state that 'the self' I refer to is the place within you connected to source, as I call it. You may call it the universe, higher self or God. It doesn't matter so much what you call it, the self is the place inside each one of us that holds complete wisdom and oneness to all things. I encourage you to trust in the wisdom of self for the answers you seek, and don't worry, I will show you exactly how to do just that. Once you decide you are willing to lean into yourself with the support of source all around you then there is really no stopping you.

LET'S BEGIN

A journey of awakening is sparked by a deep desire for change, usually from something you have experienced. It may come in many different forms, perhaps a relationship break up, learning from your past, a sudden illness or an accident that forces change upon your life to name a few.

More often than not this desire is first found along what feels like a deep, dark, scary path into a never-ending hole. You get sucked into its bottomless pit like a familiar anchoring and when you sink all the way to the depths of what's calling for the change, you feel with every fibre of your being that you cannot take it anymore. A decision has to be made because you can't possibly wallow in these suffocating depths any longer. It doesn't feel good to you because it is not in alignment.

You start to realise you are being redirected to choose differently, again and again.

I have been in this dark hole that swallows you up and calls you to the innermost places inside yourself, resulting in the experience of lower vibrations such as despair, fear and doubt. It can feel as though you are completely stuck and drowning at the same time. The familiarity within these cycles leads us to continuously dive to the uncomfortable depths until we are ready to break free. At first we may choose circuit breakers to create space for different choices, then eventually our thoughts and beliefs can change, over time, with practice.

Confusion can live in every tiny crack and crevice of change, especially when just beginning to transition from old to new thoughts, beliefs and actions. This is because you haven't previously had the experiences to provide you with the clarity and that's okay. You aren't always meant to know and if you really feel into it you may not have ever lived out a situation that's allowed you to embody a new experience just yet. How are you supposed to know how to live differently when it's not been part of the known before? It needs to be created by you, for you.

You may be wondering how you got here, why it's all changing, feeling overwhelmed and possibly asking "why me?"

How did this all come to be this way for you?

Please know that you are not alone.

Over time you may have allowed your power to slip away from you in situations that served you at that time, or allowed parts of what feels like your identity to be stripped away by each disappointment you experienced and never spoke up about. It's from the depths of this place that change becomes inevitable. That place where you have truly had enough of the old way, so a full embodied decision is made to start a journey back to self, to go inward, to who you were before any of these experiences happened to you.

There may have been so much you have allowed up to this point that you feel you can no longer live through the same experience again. Perhaps you have been at this breaking point many times, each one creating a new depth of heartbreaking guilt, shame, blame, sadness and despair until it becomes so unbearable you know to the very core of your being this is the final straw. Understanding that everything you have experienced and been shown through your unique programming and conditioning up to this exact point has in fact played an important part in your journey.

Intergenerational patterns of behaviour will play out and it's inevitable that certain traits will be passed down through lineages waiting for someone to break the chain and set the bloodline free. It's not an easy task to take on the breaking of these cyclic ingrained behaviours that are stored within the DNA of each and every one of us, being all we know until we discover there is a new way. For those of us who came here to heal these patterns, something usually happens that forces us to look at it from a different perspective, whether it be trauma or an upheaval we cannot control, until a decision to change from a place of complete awareness rises from within. From our soul.

You will feel this decision resonating through your entirety —heart, mind, body and soul. The calling to choose differently for yourself is here right now, and through the confusing fog of the past you will decide if this is the time you make one of the biggest decisions you may ever make in your life—to let go of all you have known and choose an unchartered way forward.

The unknown seems scary but so do the exhausting, continuous challenges that swallow your identity whole and leave you gasping for remnants of hope, as you keep finding your way back to yourself whenever you ignore the signs. Each time losing another piece, each time becoming a little more distant to your true nature. The unknown is asking you to unlearn all that you have been shown and choose again as you let go of your grip on the old stories, which are holding you in a place of suffering so long as you are attached to them.

These old stories have served you, maybe even protected you and helped you survive. They led you to the path you are now on so choosing to let them go isn't a small feat. Seeing the learnt behaviours and stories you were programmed with in their truth will help you to shed them. Stepping outside of the stories that happened to you so they become impersonal allows you to delve into the sweetest sense of freedom as you liberate yourself from each one. This is the decision to choose again, as an individual led by a centred self.

Choosing a new way forward for yourself is a process of rebirth which can bring an uncomfortable phase of life that feels like a full purge of your system. The realisations of things you need to feel deeply to be able to let go of can be intimidating and you may feel like running away from them. But there is also so much joy, love, happiness and gratitude that follows authentic choices. It is a beautiful awakening to a new awareness you didn't have before. And once you see, you simply cannot unsee.

Making an authentic decision is very vulnerable, knowing you have healing to do, obstacles to clear, patience to hold within yourself on the journey to an open heart. The only way forward is through it; navigating through the stories to the other side where you can just be. You know there is work to be done and that you will be choosing your path every day moving forward. When you can do this with the trauma, triggers, addictions, judgement of the self, on the bad days and on the good days, you know you are healing.

Over time you will change your perception, and you will change your world. Once you see, feel, and know that blame keeps you stuck, you will begin to search for your true identity; the one without the stories and learnt behaviours.

When we hold onto patterns we also hold emotions in our body. If we ignore and suppress them, they begin to communicate via pain, tension, injuries, or illnesses. These show up to give us a specific message and if we don't listen or witness what our body is showing us, the messages can get louder creating more stored negativity within the cells which can manifest as serious or recurring conditions. Be aware that this may become part of another story as the victim who is always sick or has chronic pain. On the other hand it may be something you can feel and be with as you transcend the emotion that was behind it in the first place.

The moment we stop running the stories, playing the roles we don't want to be playing and instead tune into our heart, we stop searching externally for our identity. We stop searching for the wisdom we desperately seek outside of ourselves through courses, books or teachers, instead learning to tune into our own inner messages and intuition, realising it is all within us. You can learn to become completely unconditional toward the self. You can learn to be governed by faith rather than fear.

Imagine you are standing at a crossroad. You see the well-paved embedded ways of the past before you, probably giving you a false sense of security and comfortability. Now see the other path you haven't walked before, which may seem scary and possibly a little exciting as you take in the uncharted territory that lay before you.

Both paths are there for you to choose. The known or the new? By seeing them and feeling what each path represents you give yourself an opportunity to choose. Whatever the choice you make, you now have a full knowing that this is what you are calling in for yourself as you take each step forward.

If you were to see yourself at the crossroad now with nothing but truth in your heart, what is the outcome of your choice?

Is it serving you?

Does it feel good?

Do you want to choose again?

What will you decide?

3

Surrender the story

> *"THERE CAME A TIME WHEN THE RISK TO REMAIN TIGHT IN THE BUD WAS MORE PAINFUL THAN THE RISK IT TOOK TO BLOSSOM."*
> *- ANAIS NIN*

KNOWING THE STORIES THAT KEEP YOU STUCK

We often try to experience growth from a place of quick fixes and spiritual bypassing, especially when we first begin our journey back to self. It seems natural to lead with the mind (time and time again) as that is where the program is hard-wired. We eventually find ourselves looping around in a cycle until the mind can carve out a new pathway to a different behaviour.

For example, you notice a pattern of constantly being rejected from job interviews. It hurts and makes you feel unworthy but instead of wanting to acknowledge the feeling you either suppress it or quieten the cyclic pattern with an avoidance reaction such as drinking alcohol, taking recreational or prescription drugs, blaming others, overachieving, or keeping busy, just to name a few.

The same pattern then shows up in new friendships or the dating scene where you are rejected again, and eventually you start to wonder, 'Why me?' 'Why does this always happen to me?' The answer is always in a pattern or form of rejection towards self, where you are likely avoiding what is behind the rejection and masking it. You may even get the job or relationship and those unworthy hurtful sensations settle but only temporarily—the rejection will manage to filter throughout your life in a cycle because you still hold resonance to it until you become aware of it. The same pattern can arrive again and again, showing up in a variety of ways. I believe it continues to come so you can eventually know it well enough to transcend it.

These stories come from somewhere, and they will keep you stuck.

Let's go deeper. Perhaps when you were a child a parent was always too busy to play, help with homework or listen to you talk about your day, which made you feel like you were constantly being rejected or not important enough. You may develop feelings of being unworthy of love and attention, which can then play out in various ways throughout your life, until eventually you come to a fork in the road where you decide you've now had enough of feeling this way. As you begin questioning and inviting in curiosity towards your own behaviour, towards the rejection you experience, you then start zooming out of the story enough to notice rejection is really just redirection, coming from a program that is old.

Perhaps you never really wanted that job in the first place, it was just what was expected of you or it ticked the boxes so you could be seen, needed or approved of by your family or friends. These realisations change your path because you get curious about the story, you uncover the root cause to what is really going on under the surface and in time begin to understand the universe is always redirecting you towards your true path—one where a force much larger than you is guiding the way. It will not usually lead you straight into your comfort zone, or in the direction of a program someone else wants for you, or what you think you need to do to satisfy the program or anyone attached to it for that matter.

I see this all the time in the work I do as a facilitator of awakening and change—there are always deeper insights offered when one is ready and open to receive them. I believe until then we go through what we need to learn, and that nothing happens by chance. Everything that has ever happened to you led you here to choose again. The difference is after experiencing expanded awareness to the program it no longer gets to define you or your choices.

Let's take a lower vibrational feeling like anger to explore now. As an example, you don't like the anger and frustration you experience when you are unseen and unheard by someone close to you. It can be overwhelming, perhaps you feel triggered by it and you just don't know why. This anger has its own story, perhaps it's the same anger you see in your mother or father, who saw it in their mother or father because for generations the parents of that bloodline never truly saw their children due to a belief that children should shut up and do as they are told.

An experience such as this will be lived out time and time again, where children of that lineage have some form of issues with their throat, self-expression, communicating their needs, making choices, or speaking up to name a few. It may even manifest as skin issues, outwardly showing a lack of approval of the self, or they may have become pushovers and people pleasers. Then those children have their own children, and you guessed it, the ancestral line keeps choosing to control with anger, passing those tribal tendencies down and unconsciously keeping them alive. It is all they know because no one has yet changed it.

By knowing the story, you are simply beginning to connect all the pieces of the puzzle. You see the fear that lights your way to the unknown way of living, which can be scary for such a deep program. The mind seems to want to have it all figured out, holding patterns and coping mechanisms that have been cultivated in times where things didn't feel so good. These patterns will live in each present moment with you, imagine them like a shadow following you around while they remain unseen and unattended.

THE ROAD THAT TAKES AS LONG AS IT TAKES (TO LET GO OF THE STORY)

Like each of us, I had so many stories. When I began the overwhelming task of piecing all mine to their origins, I started asking myself, "Is this mine to be carrying?" I felt like a walking library, with stories spilling out all over my life. I left home as soon as I could, playing out the story of the abandoned outcast of the family. I was never shown effective communication so I became a high achiever and a people pleaser, wanting to be acknowledged, loved and seen by my father mostly. The stories I was living by like a signed contract were far from my true identity, hence why I wanted to escape home—although I didn't know at the time why, nor did I have the tools to understand how I was feeling or why I acted the way I did— it was simply an inner knowing that would come sweeping in, overwhelming me from time to time, showing me that something wasn't quite right for me. I was uncomfortable being so misunderstood and I felt unwanted which of course was painful. I felt angry, like an insignificant teenager that could only be herself around her friends. This was not anyone's fault, we were all just living our own story so well. Looking back I can see this is where I settled quite deeply into victimhood.

I was strong-willed and became tired of the over-achieving to be seen story. I spent so much time in my room playing my guitar to avoid how I really felt but it was lonely, which led to me being a damn good rebel without a cause. I found myself lost in the world with nowhere to go, scared a lot of the time and feeling like I had no one to turn to.

I became a mother at the age of nineteen, which really helped reinforce my story of doing it alone in the world. It allowed me to carry the 'it isn't fair' story, embracing victimhood, complete dysfunction, and a deep sense of feeling unlovable and unwanted into a relationship that started when I was twenty.

I sabotaged everything from a deep belief it wasn't safe to be in the world. In my twenty-year-old eyes, I believed no one would want me because I didn't feel anyone ever did, so I settled into this relationship that lasted nine years. It took my stories and turned them against me in the form of manipulation and control. I was prime for the picking because I was already a victim, attracting the perfect person to reinforce my stories for me. This co-dependent relationship turned out to be abusive, isolating, and the most toxic, traumatic time I know I will ever allow myself to experience.

It was here I landed, where my beliefs were so rigidly cemented to experience a time where these painfully layered stories felt relentless and exhausting.

By the time I was pregnant with my second child at the age of twenty-five I knew I was in a very unhealthy relationship. I knew each time I chose to stay after being disrespected sealed my fate deeper, because the longer I stayed the less I knew who I was, the more disconnection I experienced to self, and the deeper I sunk. Hollow, numb and vacant are words I would use to describe the feeling looking back now.

But there is always a breaking point, and my first came when I was twenty-two weeks into this pregnancy. My partner and I were fighting about the drugs I found (that he was taking) and I knew my voice was coming alive because I had never felt so enraged in my life. Here I was again, creating the same scenario of neglect, drama and victimhood with that deep despair in the pit of my stomach—this time having a baby with a sense of no safety, stability or love present. In that moment, the feeling of getting out what I had to say was far more important to me than keeping it in, overriding any fear of the punishment I would receive from making him angry. And of course, it came.

I knew being pushed over onto the concrete, spat on and hiding in the neighbour's yard shaking in fear, petrified of what may happen if he found me, was not right. I had my eldest son I had to protect, too. I'd secretly been to counselling so I knew this relationship was controlling and toxic, but I didn't yet have the tools to cope or leave. I allowed myself to be further programmed and conditioned to what he knew as the right way to do life. And in the meantime, I needed to be wanted and needed, to be the fixer (of course I was not able to fix any of it in almost a decade of trying), so I stayed in a story of constant confusion, gaslighting, rejection, abuse, and fear, with only tiny, momentary glimpses of my true self coming through—which became fewer and further between the longer I stayed.

I wound up in hospital with nerve damage to the left side of my face and I was spotting blood only half way through the pregnancy. Safe to say I had hit an all-time low. They called the nerve damage Bell's Palsy, so I looked up my cherished Louise Hay book, Heal Your Body (I was a body worker and had done a reiki course so even though I hid the more spiritual part of myself I was still drawn to it for personal enquiry.) Bell's Palsy can be a symptom of suppressing emotions such as deep anger and rage, as I had done prior to this fight every time I couldn't speak up or was lied to and kept it all in. I was told the left side of my face would never return to normal; The small things I took for granted like drinking out of a cup properly were now gone.

So a week later I fled with my son, who was four at the time. We stayed at a hotel near a mountain, with what little money I had. Only one person knew where I was.

By this stage I had started waking up and listening, so I chose not to accept this reality of permanent nerve damage to my face. I went to acupuncture, massaged my face to stimulate the nerves daily, found things to do that made me feel calm, and only three months later had sensation back in my face.

I was still scared because at the time of leaving I was still spotting. I had to take a break from work and reassess my options, while feeling like I had none. I was so embarrassed and fearful of what others would think if I told them my truth, like I had failed. Confusion reigned and with my abandonment story so perfectly intact I struggled between feeling strong and feeling fearful of taking care of two children on my own. Only two weeks later I returned home with parts of me even more dismantled in the returning. I found the courage to tell his parents pieces of what happened before I went home, but received no help or support. In hindsight going back to the relationship after everything that happened, I was showing the deepest parts of me that I was allowing a whole new level of abuse, and in that understanding, I accepted that new depth of abusive treatment toward myself. After all it was normal to me. Through what I now know to be the cycle of violence, I was told, "I'm sorry, everything will be different, I'll never do that again, I'll get off drugs and hey let's move away and I'll sort myself out then." Like many others with this story, I wanted to believe it all so badly. So I moved time and time again, isolating myself and allowing myself to be controlled and manipulated. In the end, the abandonment stories I took on only led me to abandon my true self.

There was another story that sat just under the surface and felt so terrifying to me—the judgement of my family. I now had two kids to two different fathers, and I wanted him to be different. I wanted life to be different, and I wanted to provide a sense of home and family for my children so much that the fear of judgment at the time for me felt worse than the actual abuse. So I stayed longer. I didn't know I could provide a feeling of home and family for my boys all on my own. Over time, I became accustomed to an even more disconnected way of life. It felt so normal after a while that I unconsciously used protective strategies where I would completely close myself off to feeling altogether. I stayed for four more years, until my youngest son was three years old.

Looking back it was such a helpless time. It felt like I was digging my own deep hole with a blindfold on. If someone had uttered words of wisdom to me in those brief moments of strength I did experience, I believe I might have heard them—sometimes we don't hear anything until we are ready because we are storing so many emotions and fears that we do not want uncovered. But I was finally ready.

If by any chance you are at the edge of readiness, if you are ready to receive such a message, then from me to you right now please absorb these words into your entire being:

You are worthy of unconditional love and you are worthy of having your needs met.
It is okay to ask for help, just be careful who you reach out to, make sure they are safe and make sure they won't reinforce your story.
The blame keeps you stuck so choose you and slowly begin to let go of what's known.
Imagine the unimaginable for yourself; freedom can be yours.
Nothing you need is outside of yourself. Lean in, find you, find your inner voice and truth. It is possible.
Focus on one step at a time. One day at a time.
Everything is going to be okay.

It's going to take as long as it takes for you to hear these words, to believe they can be part of your story, to believe you can become impersonal with your story, and most importantly to be brave enough to stand up and be the one that changes the story. It takes time to follow the thread of what you discover is right for you over what isn't right. And it will take as long as it takes for you to let go of the story.

HANDING IT OVER

What is it truthfully going to take for you to surrender the story?

Well, besides a good hard look at your behaviour, it requires an understanding of your own past patterns, the inner journey of transformation, accepting that everything you create is from the present moment, knowing how impactful your belief system is and actively changing it, and understanding how internal agreements anchored in the past are no longer serving you. The mind wants to know the ins and outs of every trauma you have experienced, causing you to suffer way beyond what you actually need to. Digging into the shadows and the light, let me answer this with an honest simplicity (because let's face it the truth can be pretty damn terrifying)...

To truly surrender to your story, it is going to take a deep internal willingness.

I'm talking about the straight up willingness to change—the kind that's right on the edge of the unknown ready to jump in, with a compassionate commitment in your heart to look, to know, to feel, to go to the places that scare you and liberate yourself from the stories that are keeping you stuck.

It is helpful to understand the story is just that, a story. It has been written and lived and continued to be lived. It is all the things you were learning in childhood, the beliefs of other people that you soaked up like a sponge because you had such a curious developing mind. You were shown the way of the world through other people's eyes, learning values you thought were your own and you lived them. We go on passing these down from generation to generation until a brave soul stands up and says:

This is enough, I recognise the pattern of this and I do not need to do it anymore. This isn't my story to carry.

It's the brave soul that stands up with willingness to change and knows the story is done because it's in the past. This brave soul knows there is choice. And they begin to choose it, daily.

Sometimes that also means the willingness to reach out for help, because something so unforgivingly unimaginable happened to you and you can't move past it alone. Surrendering to the story is a transformational process—it is far from a quick fix and it is far from the comfortable realms of the known story. It's the beginning of the awakening journey into evolution and the beginning can be the most important part. That first call out for help, that first time you speak up, the first realisation that change is needed, feeling that willingness with your entire being. The first step to acceptance of what has been and the knowing that you have the power to choose again for yourself is here now.

CHOOSE YOU

From here, think of choosing again as repeated acts of choosing yourself. To be grounded in yourself, returning to the present moment time and time again because here things make more sense, and it's nicer than visiting the dark hole of the shadow behaviour unconsciously that is led by past stories.

Entering a new place of awareness because you chose to now—how liberating is that toward a new direction?

From the present moment you know yourself, you remember yourself as you were before it all happened, so who it is you choose to become in every decision you make in each moment is actually yours to own. That willingness is with you through the pain and the healing, through the dark into the light. Knowing each step from here that you are worthy of a new ending, and it is your choice through willingness into resilience and bravery to keep choosing you until it becomes an entirely different narrative for your life. It gets to become the new normal for you. What would you like your new normal to be in the coming days, weeks and months?

Can you begin to feel now that only you can choose these things within yourself?

Do you get the sense that your very freedom is within you?

It is there right now waiting to be elected as the new way. Get familiar with it. Get familiar with yourself.

The only way out is through.

THE ELEPHANT IN THE ROOM

What is Shadow work?

It is usually seen as scary so naturally it is avoided. It's the work that lives in the lower world, what's underneath the surface. Shadow work is peeling those vulnerable, hidden parts open and exploring the places we perhaps don't want to look at because they have been serving us for a time. When dancing with your shadows you may find the question of 'Who Am I' arise and this is great!

It's important to be aware firstly that there are shadows within us all, that we choose to consciously enter the work, and that it is in the darkness within us where we are able to let the light in and heal in a deeper way.

Shadow work I feel is best looked at as a way of receiving messages from a point of observation. When we can catch the unconscious behaviour and enter this space with compassionate openness and awareness to it, while keeping an eye on our needs in the process, we can begin to see where our attention and energy flow needs to shift.

Shadow work is not by any means a quick fix, it's a transformative process (as all change is) because there is embedded conditioning and programs stored so deeply in your cells, in the memories you experienced as a child, in how life has shaped you and will keep shaping you whether you choose to live unconscious to the shadow or consciously walk the path knowing all parts belong. It's not until we are ready to be honest with ourselves that shadow work can truly unfold. Not until we are ready to own our behaviour, to grieve what has been, to let go and travel to the places that possibly haven't been opened for years or most of one's life.

Experiencing lower frequencies and shadow work plays a major part in the process of growth and as we move through working with shadows it can be helpful to acknowledge one foot is in the work and one foot can be firmly planted in the present moment. Learning how to be in the now and allowing self to lead during this work allows you to remain heart centred through the discomfort that may be experienced. It's a time individually and collectively to acknowledge that there is awakening all around us, things are changing in this world and it's a time to ask, "Am I ready for a higher understanding of self, to become self-led, to see life from a new perspective, to allow space for my shadows to be there as I lovingly accept life as it is and travel through the dark gently?"

PURPOSE

Your life purpose is your contribution to this experience you are having right now. With no feeling of purpose, what sense would taking the time and effort to understand and surrender the story make, for the story has led you here, to this very moment, to live with purpose along a path of evolution.

To live in purpose is to feel an innate sense of love and belonging within and to something that lights you up. The old story and the people you absorbed information from along your path to now, all in perfect order gave you what you needed at the time, every time. Living on purpose transcends the dysfunctional stories into a gift, allowing that gift to be your purposeful message that ripples out to the world. This is you becoming the change that you wish to see reflected all around you in the external world.

Being purposeful is asking yourself, "Who am I? Who am I without the story? And how can I use my story for good?" By being in purpose you allow yourself to set a new foundational structure for the truest part of the self to shine. You hold acceptance in allowing the change, to what is going to be born from this new space you have created for yourself. So when everything feels it has broken down can you view life with fresh eyes and ask yourself "How do I now choose to rebuild this?"

Purpose can become blocked and foggy when we are living a story that isn't ours, which is why it is so important to really look within and recognise the uncomfortable things keeping you stuck. It is deep transformational work, where the shadows hold the answers even though at first that are so hard to look upon. It isn't easy and we all cycle layer by layer finding our way to live in purpose.

You don't need to go looking for purpose.

Choose you and let your purpose find its way to you.

A LETTER TO MY FEAR

Hi Fear,

How are you doing in there? I have felt you rising, I acknowledge your place but I need you to know I am choosing different for myself now. You kept me safe when I needed it most, you are strong and you helped me survive many years of pain and suffering.

I want you to know I'm not choosing to be in the anger anymore, I have created safety all around me with love and I have let my walls down which I know you didn't enjoy. Thank you for showing up again and allowing me to work with you. I know this isn't easy for you. It's been a rapid evolution lately, with constant upgrades and investment to a permanent state of expansion. I'm in it, with you.

I know I tend to go all in with wild ego stripping experiences and you have done an amazing job at showing up every step of the way. I need you to understand that in the depth of experiencing you, you have allowed me to feel the depth of joy, freedom and love too, so it's time that I let go a little more. I let you go slowly and gently to receive more light so deservingly.

Carefully showing you that hurt happens anyway and we survive together, your job of keeping me so closed and safe is now done—know I've got this. Now when I feel you I will choose to open each time, showing you we are creating a new way forward.

With gratitude, thank you for everything. I accept I no longer need to play it small, to only open to where I have been before. We are going new places now, I know you'll turn into more excitement as we go and I'll honour you each time you need me to sit with you. Know this is a very beautiful illusion. I am creating my illusion to be a magical dreamy life of ease, depth, loving awareness and pure joy so I let go of this grip, to nurture you and to receive what I am creating in its entirety.

I know you'll be back when I need you most and I'll embrace you as I choose the vast spaciousness of opening when we meet again.
I love you, thank you,
Jessie

INNER WORK REFLECTIONS

I invite you to take some time to reflect, to journal and process what has come up for you in this chapter. I have some prompts below to help you explore. Take your time and be gentle with yourself.

- Are you ready to step into your own shadows, in full support within this space and structure to navigate your way from the old to the new—knowing fully that life will change by doing this work and it will impact you and people around you as you shift?
- Knowing also that you may be triggered in this process as shadows surface and from there it's your choice to do the work, find support and integrate what you uncover and learn throughout your unique journey?
- Are you ready to self-care as much as you need through this process?
- Are you willing to step forward, to be seen, and to allow yourself to thrive? This means you have to be open to receiving.
- Are you committed to staying aligned to your heart, to the power of your own heart knowing through heart connection we have the ability to rise again after times of heaviness?
- Why are you choosing to dive into the shadow work, what part of you wants the change? This is important to

get clear on before we start so you can reference back to it. What change do you seek and why?
- Write a letter to your fear. Use my example if you need help but change your feelings and experience to it. Then read it out loud.
- Sit in meditation, ground yourself, and repeat the mantra I AM as you breathe easy.

Slow down your racing thoughts

See me, breathe with me, I am here
Forgive the ones who taught you obligation
Let go, choose with me, I am here
Feel the old leaving and use it to fuel the fire within
Light up, dance with me, I am here
Stand firm in your freedom
Be held, unfold with me, I am here
Keep a safe space and know it will open
Receive it, discover with me, I am here

-Jessie Moss-

4

Invitation to heal

> *STAYING VULNERABLE IS A RISK WE HAVE TO TAKE
> IF WE WANT TO EXPERIENCE CONNECTION.*
> *- BRENE BROWN*

GOING DEEPER

After what is usually a process of many trying times delving through the layers of surrender, learning the patterns, the stories and the cyclic behaviours of what has been, you learn to accept them and make the necessary changes on the path forward. It is helpful to recognise this can be a mentally and emotionally draining process.

The mind takes time figuring it all out, and it loves to run wild with a good old story along the way. Stories that can lead to feeling like you are taking one step forward and two steps back. The mind is busy placing the pieces of the puzzle together, relearning and rewiring, and sometimes it requires being open to receiving help in the process.

We can work a lifetime on an act such as forgiveness, that our brain tells us we want and helps us to speak. It will show us how to achieve it too, usually along a comfortably mapped out path, only to find this path has blocks along the way. Let's get comfortable knowing that there is no right or wrong way to travel your path and that the mind's known way is not the only way—chances are it is choosing a familiar way you might have tried previously because it feels safe, but it may just be time to try something different.

You will reach a point where you begin to feel the unhealed parts of yourself, the parts that more than likely link way back to the child inside you that never received attention, care, love, safety or whatever it is that you long for in this life. Such stories from the past that surround us and swallow us up, constantly robbing us from our present moment choices that are so imperative to continue on an authentic journey forward.

There is always a specific moment where my clients say, "That's it, I'm done now, I see all of it much more clearly and I'm choosing to have no more of this. This time I have had enough, I'm willing to do the work." And at this exact moment they let go of carrying the load—whether part of it, all of it or just a brief brush to pick it back up again. This is the crossroad of choice. Eventually we will choose differently before we get to exhaustion, despair or anger. And we learn that it can take many times to arrive and choose before we transcend past it.

We choose to return to self again, usually when we receive all we have learned from the lesson involved. It comes when you can't take the abuse anymore, when you have an illness from the resentment and unexpressed anger you've kept inside, or when no matter how hard you try sometimes you find yourself sucked into the vortex of story again. And that's okay. It takes practice, like learning to ride a bike. We don't always transcend the things we have lived for years or even a whole lifetime in one choice alone; it is an accumulation of each and every decision and the commitment to them with embodied actions that are in alignment with the new way forward. This is why it feels hard; it is unknown. Shifts occur throughout life by clearing what no longer serves you. It is completely life changing and it takes energy, patience and willingness.

Once the truth begins to be uncovered layer by layer, we may find we cannot heal it without sensing the feeling or emotion attached to it.

MESSAGES FROM THE BODY

In thirteen years of working as a massage therapist and tuning into bodies, I found myself exploring what was behind the recurring injuries I was treating. I wondered what was really blocking my clients from gaining full movement in mobility and the easing of their pain. Everything led me right back to Louise Hay's book, Heal Your Body. The more I worked with people the more I began to feel what the body was saying. I would look it up for clients that were open to it, always so fascinated at how powerful the messages were and the healing it created when the client was willing to look under the surface of the physical.

I had my own injuries and illnesses to overcome, too. For example, I suffered with chronic lower back pain for three years and had countless treatments from physio's and other massage therapists I was working with. I had scans that didn't give me answers, I sought advice from other personal trainers and movement specialists, doctors, chiropractors, osteopaths, and kinesiologists— I even looked into my hormones and gut health. I was forced to cut back on teaching Pilates and yoga because the pain got too much, and then I had a miscarriage when I landed in a loving relationship of three years which made it all so much worse. It became very clear I was storing a lot in this part of my body and it hadn't been safe for me to feel —- until it was.

I had seen every therapist I could think of and read every article on pain, but nothing was changing; I had to lean into the feeling behind my pain. So, I slowly began to allow myself to feel it. I felt the holding pattern when I tuned in and sent breath to it. I was desperate to move properly without pain, and I began noticing when my back would flare up. After so much searching I decided to exercise again and follow my intuition while being in my body each day. I started breathing and relaxing into my lower belly and back where the pain was and I began noticing how tightly I was holding it. Eventually I had to make the choice to feel it in its entirety. I was over it. The pain and suffering once again had brought me to a crossroad.

My mind figured it all out—it was a fight or flight response, holding onto unexpressed trauma. I was holding the pain of constantly handing my son over to someone I felt was incredibly toxic, and it was still making me sick years after getting out of the abusive relationship. I would notice every time I had to go to court whether it be for divorce, domestic violence, or the family court that my back would completely seize up. So, with the knowledge I gathered over those three years, exhausting all avenues and spending a lot of money getting others to fix me, I decided I would heal myself.

I felt all of it, like a heavy weight from years of carrying the burden of shame, blame and incapacitating pain. I had to process what I was holding onto which was enormously overwhelming. I chose to take steps towards letting go of the story I was clinging to while I waited for justice through the court system, which placed my energy and power outside myself and in other people's hands. The justice that seven years later still hadn't arrived. I can't begin to imagine the effects on my work, life, children and my own body if I was still waiting today. The truth was the impact of my situation had already worn down and sabotaged a loving relationship because of how much I was holding, unable to go to those places to let it go. It had taken a big enough toll on my life already.

This journey into the body where we begin to feel and trust the connection with our inner world is different for everyone. All the anxiety I decided to store in my lower back for me represented the trauma of a time I had been unable to let go. Accessing my breath and feeling this chronic pain was mind blowing for me at the time—it's like I was hearing my pain's story, feeling just how much was in there and when the time came I listened to all of it.

By tuning into my body, I began to release the deep sadness, guilt, lack of forgiveness, and all the trauma experienced during a toxic relationship that was residing within me because I allowed it to make a home there. With time and commitment to my daily practices, I was eventually able to experience a calmer life, returning to the basics of movement and developing a trust in my body I never had before. I started the beautiful journey of feeling safe in my body again. I thanked my body for the messages, feeling so grateful that I was able to get out of my head and into my body because it created so much healing. It felt like a deeper, tuned-in healing than everything else combined that then rippled throughout my entire life. To this day, I experience no lower back pain at all. I have gone on to heal other ailments within my body and even avoided surgery so I can wholeheartedly tell you healing from within ourselves is absolutely more than possible.

TUNING IN

When we take ownership of our pain and really listen to it by being present with it in our body, we can then truly choose to stop punishing others for what we carry, and stop expecting others to heal us. The unhealed parts of you are not who you are unless you let them define you. And you are definitely not here to hold onto pain and suffering. I know that might feel hard to read but isn't it good news that we can work on healing rather than be busy holding on!

Dropping into connection with your body to feel and heal isn't always easy, but neither is the way of suffering or pain. Tuning into connection may be uncomfortable and quite an emotional time, and you may not always get an answer or explanation of why this message is in the body.

As with my experience of chronic back pain, there was so much searching, blaming and focusing on my pain for so long because I had to know reasons with my mind; I wasn't connected to myself enough at that time to be able to fully listen and I sure as hell did not want to feel any of it. The journey, however, led me back to choice. The pain became louder than whatever I was carrying so eventually I looked deeper as we so often do. We wait until it's bad enough to make a change, holding on right to the end of our own capacity and exhausting ourselves only to realise that the entire drawn-out process actually kept us in the suffering.

We are not always meant to know the answers, but we are continuously encouraged to tune in and connect, not just to the thoughts, but to the feelings, beliefs and attitudes that affect us, and sooner or later we receive the messages. The body never lies, and as Van Der Kolk's book states 'the body keeps the score.'

FINDING CONNECTION TO FEELING

This can be a scary concept for some that aren't yet willing to feel, even though as humans we are wired for connection. For some it comes easy and others it's not so easy. Either way, this is a vital part of your healing. In connection with ourselves and others we know who we are, and we learn who we are not. True connection deepens the moment, inspires change and creates necessary experiences you need to learn along your path of evolution.

Connection can run so much deeper than talking and sharing common interests. True connection can happen without words; it is an energy exchange between people where you are truly seen and it can be with someone you don't even know, like when you feel your energy grounded when you are with the trees, or the peace and awe you feel when you witness a sunset. We can also be with people we know well and not feel connected at all—perhaps either person isn't fully listening or are just listening purely to respond. Connecting with how you're feeling means being in the moment, sharing that smile with a stranger, and showing up as your most authentic self instead of trying to please others. It's finding connection to your body via the breath or movement.

If you cannot connect to yourself fully, how is anyone else meant to connect with you fully if that's what you desire? If you wish to connect in a different way, perhaps a more genuine way, then you will need to go within to feel who you are because that's how you will know what your needs are. This may include working on your self-esteem and learning to love the parts of you that you have hidden away, by embracing your gifts and feeling trust within yourself. It all starts from a very internal place. I know it might seem like a lot at first hidden underneath, let's call these initial non-feeling parts, knowing these parts may feel frightened to really connect. By taking one step at a time through each layer, holding patience as you feel your way into your healing, there is a whole new way of operating in the external world that opens up and its right at your fingertips.

This new way of choosing to live changes relationships from what they have been to how you would like them to be, to what is in alignment with you. By seeing yourself you allow others to see you. Awareness within opens to the mental chatter, allowing the search for reasoning to subside through trusting yourself enough to feel what's behind the situations you've created in the external world. With a broken heart, for example, your partner may have left you, and deep down you know it is the right direction for both of you but the actual unhealed part that feels so heavy for you can be the abandoned child within that is desperate to be wanted, safe, held and seen. This can feel so much worse when that part is experiencing what it did as a child, and sometimes you may wonder why it feels so hard to get over but grief takes time, and maybe the unhealed wound has you focused on how much you are always abandoned or not good enough therefore being in the old patterns cause you to miss out on what's in front of you right now—nonetheless it is always a great opportunity to go within and heal those parts of yourself. The sooner you are vulnerable toward seeing, feeling, and honouring these deeper wounded parts of you the more you will have your needs met because you will know what you want and need from within.

Your new sense of feeling and connection to yourself allows you to ground in your breath and body, then to the present moment where you can know the story without it defining you anymore. You can feel an uncomfortable sensation, name it to tame it, and choose the path of least resistance for yourself.

ATTUNEMENT

If you are feeling divided toward a decision or situation it may feel like you are at odds with yourself. It can be a confusing time trudging through the sticky parts of change and transformation. Once your energy attunes to coherence it begins to connect to the flow of life where there is a deep sense of trust, surrender, and a knowing that everything needed to take place that way for you to be here now. To feel life rather than just live a program that was designed to be passed down from the people before you.

Gathering the intellect from the mind and then feeling the emotions within the body attunes you to a state of being that is in alignment to your true nature because you begin to realise you have the choice to choose again through present moment awareness. You realise everything that has taken place has been an important stepping stone to embodying your true nature, who you were before the hurtful relationships, and who you are without holding the resentment and pain from childhood.

In transcending our stories around guilt, shame, and blame we find a lighter way to live. We can rediscover play, which can mend so many unhealed parts of ourselves. Once you create space, no matter how hard it seems you can begin to build a new foundation. You rebuild and create life from feeling what it is you want for yourself, so on that note be mindful as you fill the spaces you create your future from and what you align to as you move forward.

BRINGING AWARENESS TO THE BODY

I felt to place a little disclaimer in here incase you are listening to this book I do not recommend following along for this next piece. Pause and come back to it later.

Let's take a moment here to restore your body to spaciousness with your breath. Simply begin to notice your breath as you are reading this now, following it down through your body to the earth, connecting and resting here while you ground yourself. Where is your inhale landing in your body when you first tune in? Can you feel into an expansiveness within your body as you breathe in? Make some space in there.

Start to feel whatever shows up for you as you breathe here and now. Is there any gripping or holding you can breathe out? Begin to see where the breath now wants to travel within the body without changing or forcing the breath, just keep noticing it. Moving it in and moving it out. This is a simple and beautiful way to become present and to land in the body.

Once you feel present, I invite you to continue by scanning the body with your awareness, allowing the awareness to come in with each breath and feel the parts of your body that call for spaciousness. Perhaps some places feel sensations such as pain, tension, or numbness. There is no right or wrong to what you feel, so breathe there a little while now. Take your time in observation.

Notice if arising sensations may be linked to an event, an emotion, a holding on or a painful part you have exiled at some point in time or are still trying to manage. For example, the pain in your shoulder that has been there since you had a relationship breakdown can show you what burdens you may still carry. The heaviness in your chest might feel like a heartache you didn't know was still lingering.

Invite curiosity in with the breath. Spend some time breathing into what you feel, breathe space in and invite a sense of support to surround you, keep exploring and giving the feelings complete acceptance to be there as they share their messages with you. Accept your energy as it is and again, take your time here to simply observe.

Now tune into your thoughts, giving the thoughts complete acceptance for as long as you need, not asking for anything to be different, just being here with yourself. What are the quality of the thoughts showing up? Accept and notice that these thoughts become energy, a signal you send out to the world that will be creating your future. Notice if there are any thoughts you would like to invite to shift? Breathe into what shows up for you.

Become aware of feeling what it means for you to bring your thoughts and energy to rest, bringing awareness to your heart and inviting that awareness to settle calmly into the present moment, allowing love to enter and flood your entire being while you begin to feel you are already whole just as you are, and in this very moment the self is peaceful. Feel peace. Be here enjoying the feeling of being grounded to the earth below and the space all around you for as long as you wish.

INNER WORK REFLECTIONS

- What did you notice as you just went through the previous chapter by bringing awareness into your body? Write down your experience.
- Write down a daily practice commitment that you are willing to do to the best of your ability. Start small and make one commitment to self now; For example, it might be that you journal for five minutes every morning for this week or take yourself for a walk around the block.
- Take some time and journal for as long as you wish with your awareness on how you feel in this moment. Start with the words "I feel" and see what follows.
- The unhealed parts of you are not who you are unless you let them define you. Knowing that all parts of you belong, knowing some parts are louder when there is newness arising but there is always reason for it. Check the old stories you tell yourself and see if you can create a new story in its place. For example- Old story: I'm not good enough. New Story: I am worthy of a loving relationship. Be gentle with the stories, dance with them in curiosity and create some new stories now to work towards throughout the coming chapters.
- Feel into creating something that brings you joy and a sense of play. It could be art, creating a playlist, dance, make music, write a poem, go for a surf or something

you find fun. See if you can invite creativity in, again just start small and keep it simple.

Among the trees

By the breeze,
Release feeling unwanted
Release not belonging
Let fear unravel itself from any scarcity of lovingness
Breathe, Stand firm on Earth
Ask that she take away all the times
you never felt safe, receive her nurturing
Float away, Ask the ocean to cleanse you and love
you as deep as it can, Then feel it,
Allow fire to purify the mind from patterns of struggle
Sit in stillness,
Fly away with air under wings to be reborn.
Liberated in spacious truth
Spirit whispers
"Another version of becoming dear one,
be with the grief arising... you are rising".
Feel it, See it.
Weave it into every fibre of existence deservingly.
You are already Free.

- Jessie Moss -

5

Call your power back

> *PLACING THE BLAME OR JUDGMENT ON SOMEONE ELSE LEAVES YOU POWERLESS TO CHANGE YOUR EXPERIENCE; TAKING RESPONSIBILITY FOR YOUR BELIEFS AND JUDGMENT GIVES YOU THE POWER TO CHANGE THEM.*
> *- BYRON KATIE*

THE SELF

The Spiritual essence of Self is expansive; it relates to space and connection to everything. To oneness. We can move from our mental thought patterns to feeling into the body and then to accessing present moment awareness. It can bring in the alignment to Self, Soul, Spirit, Source, God, Universe—whatever you prefer to call it.

To think there is only one layer of existence and not access a full experience is an injustice to the self. All can be explored in such a beautiful journey or rollercoaster ride to the self by humbly returning home to the place within you over and over again. Moving through layers of learning in your own unique way is a blessing to the self and everyone around you.

The universal plan, belief in karma, blueprint of existence, whatever you call this adventure you are experiencing right now, will ask you to find your path and choose it. The path is your unique alignment to the self, a place that feels authentically home to you every time you choose it, allowing you to feel free—like the expansive, wonderfully awesome light being that you truly are.

Choosing the self is a complete honouring, and time and time again will provide you with nothing but magic. Is it always easy? No. I am not here to make this feel easy, comfortable or something it is not. But can it be easy? Yes.

If you actively choose your unique alignment toward the innate inner knowing of *you*, things show up in all ways, shapes, and forms that are exactly what you need in each moment.

Your values might start to change, causing how you show up in the world and relationships to be different. You may even encounter a life-changing event, or simply find yourself in a yoga class one day literally feeling like you have been found and then boom, things are suddenly different. You might find people, places, and synchronicities showing up that teach you and lead you to more open awareness and life changes; this is when the choice to know the self becomes deeply present.

So often we are shown to conform, to find structure, to follow systems that are in place as if that is the path, and we are taught not to question it.

The self is you, beyond the mind, beyond the body, beyond all of your reference points to what you think you are or have to be. It is beyond all the experiences that have happened to you, and beyond time and space. It is way out beyond our wildest imagination.

The self is the part of you that is everything and nothing all at once, and when chosen will show you this experience is an incredibly necessary speck of divine universal unfolding that will all make sense when it's supposed to. But most of all the self ever so delightfully shows us to sense wonder in the simple things and to choose grace.

Take a moment to feel just how expansive you are. Feel grateful for this very moment.

RELATIONSHIP TO SELF

How well you know yourself has a lot to do with being in your own energy and power. If you avoid being alone, have unkind thoughts towards yourself and lack self-esteem then your relationship inward to yourself needs attention. The relationship to self is linked to your personal thoughts, feelings and actions toward self-worth, self-esteem, self-doubt, self-identity, self-empowerment, self-confidence, and the self-belief that is stored within you.

To develop a relationship to the self is an absolute honouring to yourself, from yourself, and it's from this place you can call your power back. At times throughout life your energy can be plugged into people, places, ideas, beliefs, or attachments. You can unconsciously give your power away when you still have attachments or feel strongly about a person or event from your past, which causes energy to leak from you to that place or person. In the spiritual world we can intentionally cut energetic cords to remain in our own energy. Some of the signs can be feeling tired or fatigued, or not quite feeling yourself. If you are tired all the time begin to check how much of yourself you are giving out to others or situations.

Energy is in constant motion. If you are continuously giving it out you are giving yourself, and I mean literally—because we are energy. When you begin to call your power back you can feel the energy return. It is easy enough to call your power back, the next step is to move into a space of making choices to then keep your energy strong. It's your energy to call back, and it's your energy to keep strong if you choose that.

WHAT IS POWER

The word 'power' always had such a negative connotation for me. I felt that powerful people were selfish, arrogant, and aggressive but that was just from the life experiences I had up to that point. Imagine a scale of power if you will. At one end you have a people pleaser that doesn't claim much power in the world, and although they might do things to get their personal power recentred, it can go straight back out when the behaviour returns and they end up trying to please everyone around them. Each people pleaser has a story too, often seeking outside approval to feel needed or loved. They possibly felt that way throughout their whole childhood and have been carrying it for some time.

At the other end of the scale is more of an aggressive person that gobbles up all the power around them, and guess what, they are running a story too. Perhaps they never had attention from a parent or the only attention they got from them was disapproval. Perhaps they were bullied so they grew up doing that same thing to others thinking it was normal behaviour. They may be closed so there will be a lack of energy supply and love, and they will get it any way they can. Sometimes at any cost.

Can you see that we are all making choices day in and day out to have our needs met? And not always making choices from conscious places.

This stuff shapes who we are, and how we show up in the world.

A people pleaser who chooses to call their power back to themselves will begin to feel liberated. They will feel energy within their system again and be able to set loving and firm boundaries in the world. They let go of victimhood, and although they reclaim their power they won't take advantage of others because they know firsthand how that feels. Reformed people pleasers who stand in their own power will no longer seek validation outside of the self.

An aggressive bully who softens their barriers and comes into their heart can choose to harness power and strength through vulnerability. They will find they too have so much more energy within their system when they no longer need an external source to get it from and constantly chase, they will no longer panic about power supply running out as if there is not enough to go around. Their entire system will be more regulated, and they will not need to use tools of aggression or manipulation as they receive more of what they need naturally rather than forcing, controlling and exhausting themselves in the process.

I believe calling your power back is simply an act of empowering the self.

AN EMPOWERED SELF

An empowered self walks the road of personal development. They can look at themselves and make changes in alignment with their values, whether that be working on self-worth issues or addictions used as distraction. They take control of their own life from the inside out, understanding that they cannot control anything outside of themselves. An empowered self makes positive choices to keep their energy strong. These choices change their entire world and have the ability to influence everyone around them in the process.

Of course, like every journey we take there can be obstacles and tests that may arise along the way and a big one when we start to really know ourselves, when we reach this phase of calling our power back, is that it can be hard to maintain consistently. Sometimes we can unconsciously be afraid of our own light or potential. Self-sabotage can kick in and you may find you pull out all the stops to not be the powerful being you truly are. Know that anything that comes up to be addressed during this time is simply for you to acknowledge and be with —to make space for all parts of you to exist rather than push away because then you allow yourself to heal from the wound or core place by essentially letting yourself see your whole self.

The key to stepping into the powerful being you are and to standing in your light is to recognise your power isn't over others, it isn't in controlling, comparing or anything external at all.

True personal power lives within each and every one of us when we take those actions of self-care, learn to say no, forgive or choose love over fear. Personal power lives in the aligned choices we make in each present moment when we choose to turn inward. It is only when we go within that we will feel the infinite, unlimited powerful source of energy available to us all.

And from the empowered self we choose to honour self and all that is, along with all that has been.

PERSONAL POWER

Firstly, I want to point out that your will can drive you to absolute exhaustion if it's the busy mind chatter that is steering you through life from a state of constantly doing. However, when your will is harnessed towards what really makes you feel alive and empowered, what you can achieve with boundless energy will be awe-inspiring. Personal power can move you from a state of doing in those mental realms of programming, story, and distraction to discovering how powerful it is to simply *be* your true identity.

Accessing your willpower through enthusiasm comes from the act of feeling worthy and in your empowered state of aliveness. Directing willpower from a place of knowing yourself and keeping your energy strong has the capacity to create a huge amount of change in your life.

Clearing what no longer serves you from your life is an act of empowerment in calling your personal power back. In a world that seems to be encouraging more and more personal power to be stripped away, clearing yourself of programs to deeply know your true identity is freeing to the self. You will or may have already felt it is time to conform to no other system but your own internal compass of truth. It doesn't happen overnight, but it will occur through a string of aligned choices, actions, events, and embodying a new way to show up because you choose to work on building that trust and power within you—unapologetically whole already, as you are.

This doesn't have to be a scary or big thing. Take it step by step. All change starts somewhere, and small steps towards clearing those beliefs, stories, and behaviours that no longer work for you will allow you to make choices that keep your energy strong, to be true to the self, integrate as you go, and to connect with that internal fire inside. This will create a future from a place of peace with what is, rather than fear in what could be.

What choices can you make today that will make a difference in your life?

We change the world by changing what we can within ourselves.

What's happening around you is happening within you...
You are more powerful than you know.
Please remember that.

DAILY PRACTICE OF CHOICE

Never underestimate the immense value of choosing to call your power back daily, to choose yourself, and to choose a new way to live. That's what it takes when you have trauma responses showing up, triggers active, a body that needs regulating, or emotional work presenting itself that may be requiring a lot of energy. Or when you are holding pain and hurt so old, you have been in suffering so deep you may wonder if you will ever get out. I know it can feel like a lot and I invite you to acknowledge that too. You may dip down the dark hole of past memories into victimhood, addictions, and unhealthy coping mechanisms until you choose something different—there is no telling how many times we might dabble in the shadows until we understand what's up. So this requires making those new aligned choices every time the opportunity shows up, every time you become aware of it, and to act with love for self and tune into the good you have done rather than condemning yourself every time you falter.

To be in a daily practice means you are learning to trust and become familiar with the self. To create that sacred space with self. You acknowledge there is work to be done and you surrender constantly to the present moment. If you don't surrender, the path looks the same. The same feelings of anguish and fear wait like a spiral out of control and you lose the grip on direction and feelings of purpose. I know I sometimes still visit this place briefly, where I can sometimes want to give up— each time with practice the visits get shorter, each time it gets easier to come back home to myself, and each time I return a little more healed and awake.

To use myself as an example, there is part of me that can feel unsafe in the world and she needs my attention from time to time. I can know with my mind that I have been through events that I've chosen for myself because the belief was there from when I was a sick infant that it isn't safe to be here in my body. This belief developed young and caused me to learn a behaviour where I dissociate as a coping mechanism when

I feel unsafe, which means I abandon that part of myself that needs me in that moment. If I did that with one of my children if they said "this doesn't feel safe" I could imagine a response of dissociating would rattle them even more, and in fact show them it is not safe. As their mum what I would do for them is be present for them, make eye contact, and ask them what they need right now to feel safe. I would hold them and comfort them, but I wasn't doing this for parts of myself still living in the unconscious. I now choose to bring light to any parts of myself when I discover them. Those parts hold the pain, suffering, abandonment, and unworthiness to name a few. I get to know them, how they are feeling and I bring the adult mum part of me forward to give them what they need now, to soothe them, to feel it all. This is how I show up for myself and I believe this really helps me stay in my energy and sense of power.

I have accepted that certain parts of myself that feel uncomfortable exist, that they have been there a long time, parts of me can still be holding onto fear, doubt, and a sense of distrust in people from long ago. The more I can visit the scared part when I do have feelings of being unsafe, to really give it space and not push it away (even though feeling the anxiety, fear, and sense of being unsupported is not comfortable) I can show this young part of myself that I see her, I am here for her and I am choosing safety for us now. I let that part of me that still holds the belief it's not safe that I have her back and I choose safety. I show her through building trust with my aligned actions and checking in. I know the thoughts now, I can sense the feelings rising and I hold my hand on my heart and stop. I ask, "What do you need to feel safe right now?" The answer might be to have a difficult conversation and ask for my needs to be met, or to not go into the ocean when it's too wild. It is then so important for me as the adult living in the now to really show up and teach that part of me it's okay to feel it, I'm here with her to heal it, and that we are safe now. If this part knows, feels, and sees I am embodying the mantra it is safe in my body, then I bring healing to my past, peace to my present, and a new way of being safe in the world into the future I am creating.

My point being alignment needs to be chosen regularly to make an impact, which is not always easy, depending on the story and how deep it has played a vital part in your existence so far. It is hard to remember you are not who the story shaped you to be when you are angry at having to survive it daily. Or when you feel alone, like no one can hold space for it and you don't want to yourself either, but it is in fact the life you are living.

So dear one, I ask you now: How tightly do you want to keep holding onto a story, and how willing are you to set that thing on fire with glorious passion to live, freeing yourself with a daily practice of choosing something new for yourself?

You need to want it enough that you will burn the story with complete acceptance and compassion toward the self, other people, and the events that happened to you, perhaps even for holding it for so long, and walk through the process gently. You will be asked to practice the surrender of it every time its unwelcome knock comes to your door. And to embrace it with open arms.

The truth is you can't run from it, but you can learn to change the impact of it.

One choice at a time. Moving through it.

MAKING THE CHOICES THAT KEEP YOUR ENERGY STRONG

If you can right now, just feel into and own the sensations of what feels light and heavy *specifically* to you. And by this, I don't mean thinking what feels right or wrong or going into any outdated ways of yesterday. The key word being to really *feel* it.

When you sense the feeling of light, no matter how subtle that is, you have found your yes to keeping your energy strong. You will feel a flow state follow it, maybe even relief and a lightness that continues because you didn't choose the heavy sensation. Sometimes in choosing this light feeling yes way you leave things behind, which may not feel so good at the time but deep down it comes with a knowing that it will all be okay.

When you sense the feeling of heaviness and you choose the opposite, which is light for you, it could be slightly uncomfortable at the time, but it's important to listen because you then begin to change pathways to a new way of experiencing how you respond to life, and you will be setting boundaries to what you now accept for yourself. This tuning inward is where all the answers are and where they have always been. Practice this to become familiar with your unique process of it.

Heavy feeling choices tend to be repetitive, known, and comfortable. Sometimes out of habit acting on the familiar and not tuning into how you really feel you can experience lower vibrational responses like frustration, agitation, or even the poor me reactions, possibly making others around you feel heavy too.

So, when you get your sense of light, which serves your good strong kept energy, and you recognise the sense of heavy, which does not fill your cup or make you feel good, then what is next?

You must be willing to honour those feelings when you tune in, not manipulate them into what you think is right, what others expect you to do, or how you did it yesterday. This honouring and living in feeling means we are really working with what is going to serve us moving forward. This kind of choice in your way of living is going to expand your knowledge and wisdom into wide-open spaces, and what do we do with wide-open spaces? We get to create.

What do we create?

Whatever the hell it is that you want to create!

By feeling the feeling and amplifying it, simply just like *it is already here.*

And that is how you make the choices to keep your energy strong and start to create paths of unlimited amounts of awesome with the new spaces you will very soon start to discover all around you.

Sit back, let the old fall away, reflect with gratitude, and be compassionate on this journey. That way when you open to creating something new it is going to be in alignment and of your highest good along with the highest good of everyone that surrounds you.

Welcome and get to know these new sensations toward honouring a new path.

INNER WORK REFLECTIONS

- Invitation to shift your awareness. Grab your journal and explore duality with curiosity by writing down what you feel is good and what is bad, whether it be in your life, traits you have, thoughts you have about yourself. And then be curious to where this all comes from. Don't over think it too much, just put pen to paper and let it flow.
- **Here are some affirmations to journal on:** Read each one and take note on how it makes you feel, acknowledging what shows up in the process:
- I honour the power in me. I honour myself.
- The fire within me burns through all blocks and fears.
- I release judgement of others and of myself.
- I am worthy of love, kindness and respect.
- I give myself permission to be my authentic self.
- I release myself from the past.
- Everything I need, I have within.

Take any of the above affirmations that resonate or create your own to use daily to invite new energy in. You could write your affirmation down and leave a note on the fridge or mirror to remember this practice. Say it out loud three times each day. Breathe into the body that holds you, honouring the earth below that grounds you and all that surrounds the experience of us and now.

And sometimes you gotta leave it behind...

Such a wild fire
Spitting flames into yesterday
Melting hearts
Beating upside down
Clear confusing divinity
The painfully joyous opening
What an alarmingly beautiful paradox
To be here learning it
Peeling apart inch by inch
Uncovering what was
Before conditioning touched it
And it is over before it began again
Just like that
Music plays loud
Move
Let it go
Leaving it behind
There's no place quite like it is there.
Taking that step toward centre
Settling in wholeheartedly
Here it stays
Within the open depths
Chosen entirely
And it says fuck it dive in
Powerful surrendered state
Internal and vast

OPEN

Breathing
Arriving bare feet to the earth
She holds it
And she says
"Never let anyone tell you any different"
You are nothing
And everything
And it's an honour to feel it all
To be choosing self
So another self can do the same
Walk into the wild fire
With nothing
And everything
Come out new
But first,
Leave it behind

- Jessie Moss -

6

Expanded heart

> *"I AM WILLING TO SEE THINGS DIFFERENTLY.
> I AM WILLING TO SEE LOVE."*
> *- GABRIELLE BERNSTEIN*

CONNECTION

So far, we have unravelled stories of the past, belief systems that no longer serve a higher purpose, we have danced with the mind-body connection and even called power back to self. What's next, past the knowing of your identity and all the things you have carried which are linked to your external world?

It is time to explore connection.

Part of this learning is the ability to connect to self and ask what do I need at this very moment? It is the ability to give yourself the unconditional love you may seek outside yourself, the self-confidence you may be afraid to step into or to finally experience the validation you never received. This point of connection allows you to give to yourself first, unconditionally, then give outwardly to others. When you are connected to your heart, self, and source there is a flow present and there are no limits to what you can receive. However, you must be willing and take steps towards opening to receive first without conditions, as you are. Easier said than done, right?

TO BE UNCONDITIONAL

Conditions cause instant limitation. If you tend to people-please like I once did it feels natural to want others to be happy, to want to be the fixer or to just be agreeable out of habit but it can cause you to put conditions upon yourself. For example, if you are doing something that may not be fully aligned in integrity to your values you naturally won't feel very good doing it, which could turn into having a response such as frustration because your conditioning of obligation is heavy. This may cause you to withdraw, get mad or feel stress. Another example is staying quiet to keep the peace so someone doesn't treat you badly. You are blocking yourself from your truth which limits the evolution of you. It is important to remember you do not have to wait for people around you to grow in order for you to grow, and we remember this the most when we are feeling connected inward.

To be unconditional means to act with full acceptance in your heart for everything as it is and to honour it without wanting to change it. To let go of anything blocking your divine unconditional self. If you didn't have much when you were younger or there wasn't much food in the house and you remember going hungry, you might have developed a scarcity block. Holding this will limit you by feeling scarcity throughout life in other ways like there is just never enough to go around. The universe wants you to recognise your unlimited self, it really wants to provide so much for you. The question is can you receive it?

GETTING OUT OF YOUR OWN WAY

The biggest block you can begin to clear is realising you are in fact the only thing in your own way. You need to be willing to notice what you are radiating into your very reality. What you radiate you create. What seeds you plant create the type of fruit you're going to get. You cannot plant bitter seeds and expect sweetness to arrive if you are creating from the past, the mind, from experiences, or from conditioning. Imagine if you could take a step back from it and be honest towards it all, curiously questioning with compassion what it is that you are radiating out into the world. What is frustrating you externally is really inside you. What we may judge in someone else is really a mirror deeply and directly to the self. You see, we begin to vibrate at a higher frequency when we are connected to self and the heart is where we connect. The heart is the centre of you bridging the external world to the inner world.

Everything has a frequency. If you experience a hard time, let's say around heartache, this memory then holds a frequency of pain and suffering, whether you think you hold it or not if you are still experiencing suffering around you then this frequency is still part of your energetics. You radiate suffering from your heartache that perhaps wasn't fully processed back then when it was felt, and it will show up again and again in different situations, people, places, continuing to create the frequency externally for you to see what's really within you.

FORGIVE YOURSELF

Once we begin practices to reunite into that joyous feeling of being connected with ourselves, being with nature, with others, sitting with our emotions, becoming accepting of our truth, and providing ourselves with adequate self-care, life can truly begin to shift in ways we won't see coming. You may have done forgiveness work yet so often it can look like radically forgiving everyone else, completely missing the deepest part of connection which is to forgive ourselves. Forgiving the self, for me, has been the hardest form of releasing my past because it asked me to feel it all, and for a long time I wasn't ready to do that. When we forgive ourselves we are able to let go of the holding on. It is the piece of the puzzle that is calling you the most and asking you to receive forgiveness so you can experience the deepest peace possible within you to clear away old frequencies that are no longer working for you. Experiencing a peace that can open your heart wide and allow you to connect deeper than before. It is the opening needed for big life changes. There is nothing sweeter than being willing to start the journey to forgiving yourself. And maybe you can start today, be curious about what this feels like and what this means for you from the heart.

I once carried a lot of guilt and shame from remaining in the relationship I knew was toxic for myself and my children. I felt if I did better we could have avoided a lot of the trauma. I didn't believe I had the strength to get out so I was the one who allowed us to endure it all—I really believed it was all my fault. The guilt I carried and the conditioning of blaming myself helped support my beliefs at the time that I was not good enough, so naturally after leaving I first forgave my father from where I developed those low self-worth feelings. I forgave my abuser too, but I still wasn't free of it. I would wonder how the hell I wasn't free—I had done all the forgiving, hadn't I?

It wasn't until I went to Peru that the magic of self-forgiveness happened for me. I stayed at a temple in the Amazon jungle specifically to work with Shamans. I felt I needed some kind of radical healing because to be honest at times I felt so far gone I didn't know what else to do or how to keep going anymore. I was desperate, traumatised and had been stuck in survival mode for over a decade. It was here that I found total peace of mind, body and soul. I didn't even know it was happening at the time or that it had to happen—I was totally disconnected to my heart. I had huge shields up that no one could get through, and it wasn't safe to go into the heart or be opening myself up yet—not when I was still constantly triggered in everyday life. It all shifted within one simple passing of a life changing moment that came in the middle of the jungle this night. It was a full moon so I could see what was happening around me in the ceremony, and my intention that night was to simply be present because the night before in ceremony I was launched to so many dimensions I felt anything but here on earth or able to participate. So presence felt important as an intention this day (and I also was super scared to enter anymore multidimensional rocket ships in all honesty.) One moment I will remember for the rest of my life was a lightness entering my entire being and I felt all the shame from my past and all the joy I could ever want to feel arrive at the same time. I allowed the shame and severe lack of forgiveness of myself to leave, it wanted to leave, and I cried with happiness as I realised I had found a place inside of me I had never found before, instantly knowing a great shift had taken place. A place so beautiful that no words could truly ever describe.

From then on, I knew I wanted to keep opening my heart, even when I was hurting. I imagined my broken heart as a wounded part of myself where light could enter any cracks and only open it more so I became less afraid of being hurt. I became less fearful and started living more wholeheartedly. A couple of years after my journey to Peru, because these journeys take as long as they take, I began to really embody being vulnerable, recognising its strength and how much resilience I had been shown. For the first time I felt willing to step out of my own way, to love the unlovable parts of myself. To accept unconditionally all parts of me belonged. Over time my heart opening embodiment lightened my past, it felt like it let light filter in and around me and I began to have deeper connections with people, especially with my children. I wanted to feel my emotions and was no longer totally terrified of the unknown. I started to embrace life more and more and became committed to noticing times when I would dissociate. I invited play and ease into my healing because I had a solid programming of 'Mothers have responsibility, they do not play'. Playing and a life of ease as a single mother seemed totally unreachable for me. Over time I started actually believing that anything and everything for me was entirely possible. One small shift at a time in a micro-stepping kind of way kept it simpler and more doable with fresh changes in perspective that allowed me to see and experience that life gets to happen for us, and all I needed to do was remember to stay connected to that place within.

When we connect and willingly practice living life from the heart we really can live with such fullness. We can realise all is connected and there is no separation. The beautiful thing about the heart is that it is like a bridge, imagine it connecting the external world to our inner world, allowing us to be present in this experience, to what we are creating, and to travel deeper in. When we are connecting to our inner world it radiates and filters out all around us to the external world. And how blessed we are to be here with a choice to experience this and to walk that bridge home within.

SELF LOVE

If we are aware that we internally create what we radiate in this world, would we change what it is we have been holding within us more frequently?

Choice is highlighted when you step into the knowing that you are the creator. If we are seeking a depth of love we haven't received before, how would we know we are ready for that depth of love if we haven't gifted it to ourselves, asked for it, or opened to receive it yet? People can only meet other people to the depths at which they have met themselves. So, when you meet someone and connect straight away you are feeling a resonance with this person—energy never lies. Even if you are not aware of your intuition or gut instincts you are still reading a room when you walk into it, it's how you sense someone is having a bad day—you see, feel and experience this on more than one level whether you are aware of it or not.

First learning the art of self-love is key to an open heart and heart energy is absolutely unconditional. If you cannot forgive yourself and hold compassion towards your past or mistakes or even admit them to yourself, then how can you meet someone at that depth of compassion and love? It has to be accessed by you, towards yourself first, then it will move through you to others, radiating that depth of self-love and compassion, outwardly creating it in your external world.

So how unconditional are you towards yourself? What are some of the ways you speak to yourself, nurture yourself or lean into your own internal support system—is it loving there?

I like to be and converse with the parts of myself that need attention. For example, through EMDR (Eye Movement Desensitization and Reprocessing) therapy I have learnt to call meetings to open up the floor to any parts of me that are present, struggling, or needing to be heard. I see this as a form of self-love towards those parts of myself I once exiled and suppressed. For example, when I notice I am harsh towards myself, the inner critic goes to town on one of my closed parts. I remember the therapist saying to me, "You are a loving mother, so you could try and speak to some of these parts of yourself the way that you would speak and be with your boys." This, I can tell you, worked for me. When we soften to these harder parts of ourselves, the parts that believed they were unlovable or damaged discover they deserve better, that it wasn't their fault, that they can heal. They also feel it's safe to see them and work with them in this present time, that we have grown up, that they aren't damaged and unchangeable or unworthy of being free. I see it as a belief that was written into our contract and the creation of it was assisted by an external source, usually a source or pattern that was within the family structure in earlier life. These parts of us sometimes just need to be walked through a process of knowing their job is done, they are no longer alone, the painful memory is recognised and held with love and healing moving forward. I began to powerfully realise that I could be self-led. Once these parts of self are welcomed and acknowledged they become much easier to work with, and I find it's potent in helping me choose from a more aligned state of being in the present moment.

So, after we find stillness and connection to self, we can start to sense wholeheartedly how we show up for ourselves, and with a fuller acceptance of ourselves as we are, we learn to open to love for all parts that make us who we are in this very moment. We begin to understand that we can indeed hold that love to self and it is a very beautiful process.

All parts of you belong.

LIVING LIGHTER MOMENTS

Sometimes it is hard to see things clearly. Sometimes there is an unexpected, unavoidable, or ever-present unpleasant thorn in the side of your existence. I know firsthand how hard it is to return to a clear perspective with an open heart. It takes practice. Each time you get to practice there is usually a hurdle to overcome or some push back along the way, so remembering to thank these things rather than becoming consumed by them is crucial.

An open heart doesn't prevent pain from arising, but if we can trust it anyway and be so bravely vulnerable in those choices, then when we find ourselves drowning in painful uncertainty, we can still come back to ourselves—despite it being uncomfortable, because I mean it's uncomfortable either way, right?

Can pain be inspiration to open your heart more deeply?

Where can you replace resistance with trust?

Can you keep experiencing pain and allow the light in a little more each time?

When anger and fear arise, they can remind us of the strength it takes to be open and be a reminder of the good. Hold onto faith in these moments because it is only a matter of time before our heart opens again with the constant chipping away of lower vibrations that actually train us to know openness is the lighter choice. It can be through others showing us fear, bitterness, negativity and even hate that allows us to tune into the gift of choosing better for ourselves. Although sending these situations compassion can be tricky depending on the severity and hold the story has on us, I really do feel what matters is that we try rather than reciprocate negativity. There is still an expansion in choosing to try your best.

To be spending time and energy wishing that others be free of their suffering and that they become heart-led doesn't change their choice to perhaps suffer and in turn impart suffering onto others or you, it is outside of your control. All you can do is focus on yourself, which in turn does raise your own energy and put you in a position to lead by example. We can choose daily to be free of our suffering. We can invite curiosity about holding more compassion and love for the haters. They really do need it the most. Hate is lazy and easy.

From an unconditional space we can choose to send love often and keep our resonance clear of those lower vibrations.

There is nothing we can't hand over to the divine workings of the universe, even if it feels hard to let go in the moment.

Each step counts more than you may realise, and besides it is a choosing practice for the vast open spaces we can begin to occupy.

The choice to connect with your own heart when the embodiment process has begun, no matter your path to get there and no matter how many times you have to choose it—will feel like freedom. It is not outside of you; it is within you. Freedom can consume you every time you connect to your heart in remembering there is more to people's suffering, there is more to this experience, and you no longer have to exist with a heart half open or choose any kind of suffering for yourself.

This you can be sure of when nothing else seems clear to you. It is where you can land every time and feel at home, centred, full, untouchable, joyous. I highly encourage you to start believing that there are no limits within you.

If we cease doing things the old way to eliminate our suffering, fear may arise because we are not sure who we are without the stories. I am more than willing to find out—I see no other way for me now. How about you?

Boundlessness is not affected by ego, that is just the suffering of the mind speaking. Encourage yourself to put down what you are carrying over and over again. We can make wholehearted daily choices to dissolve all suffering in and around ourselves. You don't have to be clear all the time to hold awareness, so watch yourself dear one, become the witness and become more comfortable in the void of transition through willingness to choose living lighter moments.

REACHING OUT WITH LOVE

I was really interested to find along my heart healing journey that I, in fact wasn't being unconditional with love even when I knew so much about it. I wanted to share this story to invite more light to the shadow and as I write this, I am still in a beautiful discovery to it. When I was a child I would (as children do) reach out with love. It has become apparent to me that after so many attempts of this gesture and it being shut down and rejected that by the time I was twelve years old I really believed that love is actually conditional. That I must have to do things for love, that I had to hide parts of myself to fit in or be a certain way that is not myself, and that so sadly has been present this lifetime for me.

As an adult looking back at my relationships, I can see that I placed conditions on how far I could open to someone to avoid rejection—in return I have never felt fully understood or chosen when it comes to an intimate relationship. I found myself in a three-year relationship after my divorce that was the closest thing to unconditional love I have experienced but I was too traumatised to see clearly at that point in time, so I was never able to shift that belief in that situation. I found it mind blowing that I had so many tools and that I could date someone for six months and always find myself at that point in time where I was feeling like just an option. Always meeting men that weren't quite sure where they were at, with their energy still lingering with an ex, tied up in their work, or not sure what they want right now. Or 'I don't know if you having kids is working out for me.' Whatever it was, it became clear it was the same shit on a different day.

Now this part is important—I was allowing myself to be the option because I was being conditional with love. I had issues I was working on around feeling safe, setting firm and loving boundaries, being in my truth, wondering how the hell am I still getting this all wrong? And feeling ready and open for a relationship with generally my manifestation practice down to a tee I knew something else was there for me to see when I was ready to see it. So I got to the point where enough was enough. My heart still opened to love through every rejection. Every time I had to feel I was an option again was painful and it felt like a harsh reality, sometimes so much so I would just launch myself into my work and dream that when my kids were older I would choose a life of being on my own, travelling and expanding solo. From this you can discover I have avoidant tendencies in relationship because reaching out for love was met painfully for me over and over and over in this life.

I ended up finding this unconscious belief and emotion stored through a rather painful and scary episode in the middle of the night where I felt my stomach was going to explode. I had fevers, and passed out only to wake up dripping with sweat and vomiting. I don't usually have stomach issues so this was rare for me—I knew it was emotions coming to clear because I was travelling through an emotional time. What showed up in my body felt like I needed to really listen to it and I uncovered a belief that it's not safe to reach out with love, that I must have conditions around it for it to feel safe for me.

In the shadows was this part of me that was so shut down to really experience love. The belief that love was actually unconditional was never really felt or embodied, and as long as that remains I will always resonate this energy and perhaps stay as an option for people. It brings up feelings of not being wanted, not good enough—all the things I associated with what I knew to be true from my experience as a little girl. As this is integrated it is important that I choose myself and do the work around this if I want this experience to change for me, I feel it's important that I choose to reach out with love in small ways and begin to practice it when an opportunity shows up. To embody within myself that love is unconditional means being with the small part of myself that is so shut down and rejected, and now as a self-led adult I get to show her how unconditional love is. Integrating this also means opening to receive it back because I am not an option and I, just as you, exactly as you are, are so worthy of so much love without conditions on, near or around it.

A PERSONAL LETTING GO EXPERIENCE

I have found that these letting go experiences are not always a grand moment with fireworks, but more like a simple breath in and out, a smile, or a sigh in complete acceptance (even though sometimes I really want the fireworks!)

I am always reminded the mind is not a place I can solely live in anymore. It doesn't mean the mind won't try it on from time to time, but it never lasts long. It's too messy for me and seems so scrambled with the past, the future, and almost robotic responses behind what is spat out all over this precious life.

I find myself contemplating the heaviness of projecting what sometimes feels like utter nonsense from my mind out into the potent energy field that surrounds me. I contemplate this energy of spat out ramblings that I know will propel my life into old, outdated workings of the mind—a life I know so well already, that is not what the truth seeker within me really wants to create. It starts to feel like a total disregard of all manifested momentum I work so hard to hold, yet I can so easily start messing with the place creation itself is sparked. It is eye-opening to witness my own mind wanting to take the lead.

Knowing that I create this journey I walk, I choose not to occupy the mind's busyness and trauma responses for too long. Residing in the mind alone, in reflection feels like confusion for me, to know what comes from where, what's real, watching well-worn practiced stories and programming flying out of the mind into creation like a well-rehearsed play. One that makes me feel heavy like a forgetting of the self.

Most importantly, I realise that there is no choosing from this structured web of information that is overloaded with the residue of what has been and what it thinks into my reality. I am over occupying this space in such a way. There is nothing that serves me there now I have found residence in the wide-open spaces of strength, courage and vulnerability within my very own heart.

My heart bears scars of the unimaginable and it now opens anyway. My heart wants to close at times, and it has learnt to open more through each closing. There is light here that is felt so deeply and it ripples contagiously outward, filtering through to the very places that yearn for it. It is an unstoppable force to be reckoned with. There is no closing down of this powerful light within now. There is less of a busy mess here when I am self-led, where everything is aligned to my very own integrity and accepted. Here in the heart lives a love that is so much bigger than life itself.

So, I began to journey with a foreign concept of what it is to really feel and lead with my heart, feeling and fumbling my way through the discomfort to meet my hidden vulnerability. To meet my vulnerability with such depth scared me, and I really learnt to acknowledge my courage in all of these moments as I explored them willingly.

The things I know I need to let go of from time to time envelop my entire being and it doesn't feel good. But each layer shifts in its own time, knowing all of it is necessary to feel so it can be healed as it emerges. All arriving in the name of evolution.

Each time feelings arise and are released it feels like a new depth of completion, another step in the right direction and it begins to feel good again. The lesson is felt and there is no more guessing. There has been a choice to live from the heart, even though it is an unknown path ahead for me; I had never had one thought to do it any sooner than what I have, and that's because it wasn't the time.

Part of me needed to break fully to see I could rebuild, for there is much more I carry, and much more I will practice letting go of in these daily choices. Perhaps some don't realise or understand the depth I explore or how lonely it can be at times, but I am so grateful for accepting this unique journey that gifts me a freedom I'm not sure I would have experienced otherwise. It allows me to be in service to others, to thrive and to release victimhood from my field.

There is nothing outwardly grand in letting go for me. The grandness is internal, and it is just for me, a silent place where everything stops still and all is connected. The heart is the connector, where it all makes sense as it is, humble in its silent space-holding but extremely felt and met with wholeness.

Past the humblest silent spaces comes liberation in each surrender.

I let go just like that because worry seems pointless to the expansive light that grows inside me, a light that above all I make more and more space for. I let go because I love myself so much that self-respect called louder than anything else in these moments. I choose myself, with love.

Integrity had felt incoherent for far too long so I decided each day to stand firm in my values and the new agreements I make with myself so that this energy can shine outwardly from within me. I knew my calling was far greater than I was allowing myself to feel and experience. I was so scared of the unknown, but I knew I was evolving and there was something else waiting for me, so I let go in a beautiful, smiling heart-felt surrender towards the unfamiliar. Now and always, I am learning new depths to lean in and to let go.

INNER WORK REFLECTIONS

- Invitation to shift your awareness. Grab your journal and explore forgiveness.
- Sit for a moment and tune into these questions as you breathe easy, sitting with a long spine, strong back, soft front, and open heart. (These answers can help you find a way in and through your unique journey.)
- Do you know you are whole already?
- Can you sense that? If not, where don't you feel it?
- What fears might you have about becoming emotionally healthy?
- **Mirror exercise:** Look into your eyes every day for a week minimum and say to yourself, "I Love You, exactly as you are."
- **Self-care:** Commit an act of self-love/self-care in the next few days. Get creative if you feel yourself wanting to make an excuse to not do this, whether it be a lack of time or money. Make it easy to achieve right now, you don't have to spend any money or a lot of time on this. Start small. Connect however it feels right for you.

In my closing I choose to open.

To be open to possibilities is great
But without an open heart
Without connection
How does one receive fully?
They do not
I have been here
Telling myself stories of how open I am
Baby steps, trying new things
Not feeling fully met
Looking, searching… externally
I turn inward
I had to create safety for myself
I had to learn my insurmountable strength
To hold myself
I had to feel my worth fully
Then choose myself again and again
With arms wide open
I meet vulnerability
Feeling without thinking
Letting my inner world shape me
To be open from heart is powerful
There is no other place I can be
I have landed
I feel everything

OPEN

I express myself
I no longer apologise for who I am
I have too much love for myself
This woman I am always becoming
Did not land here softly
I have walked through fire for this
I accept to hold this open receptive heart
In my hurt and fear, I do not close
But I softly crack wider open
Nothing can close me now
Not one single thing.
Not now I have tasted this freedom
The joy of my depth swims deep within
And the depth of my joy like stars above
I am willing to feel it all
No programming required
I let go
I have arrived
With nothing but freedom
The wide open spaces of all that I am
I am Love.
You are Love too.

- Jessie Moss -

7

Truth is calling

> *WHEN WORDS ARE BOTH KIND AND TRUE,*
> *THEY CAN CHANGE OUR WORLD.*
> *- BUDDHA*

SEEK ONLY THE TRUTH, ALWAYS

When we connect to the self, the true self, we can wholeheartedly begin or deepen the experience of awakening to our authentic alignment. Again, I want to say these awakenings aren't always easy—they can be more painful, upsetting, and confronting at the beginning if I am fully transparent, but awakenings are also extremely beautiful. We have not lived in a time quite like this with such rising to the challenges of the unknown, it is a time filled with opportunities for change if you are willing to take them. When you experience living in truth you become untouchable, not worrying about what is right or wrong in the eyes of others, instead focusing on what aligns to your own journey from a present moment awareness only you can cultivate for yourself.

When you action your truth in your life you are redefining patterns and changing belief systems to match the vibration of your evolution. It is no wonder many people struggle with this truth phase of awakening, as it is the one thing that really scares us—there is so much fear of judgement and the unknown that change brings. What if we could choose our truth, live it, and allow all the old patterns, situations, and people that do not serve us to move out of our life, creating space for what does resonate with our truth? Even though there is discomfort in that there is also a spaciousness that is created in the process for you to walk a new, aligned way forward. This is when we start to really step into thriving—when we recognise our truth and what we value then commit to aligning to it with self-led actions.

The point I am making here is that no one can really give you what you want or tell you what your truth is. It is not found externally. It is up to you to feel into and know your truth, then of course to choose it.

WHAT IS MY PERSONAL TRUTH?

What do you hold onto that maybe no one hears or knows about?

Our personal truth in this moment is so potent in helping us become resilient to our past wounds and trauma. The truth when accepted fully is a vital step forward.

For example (and speaking from experience) allowing yourself to fully accept that you are exhausted from constant coercive, controlling behaviour from an ex or current partner. It doesn't mean you have to let them under your skin, it's just that in reality it has been a heavy load to carry and you have reached your limit with it. In the heaviness you have a chance to own the truth and respond, perhaps by setting a boundary and taking space rather than reacting from letting them get under your skin and into your energy field. Admitting these things can be a hard first step because it instantly allows you to zoom out in truth and you may not want to feel the truth of it. Truth as it is shows you where you have work to do if you want to change it, beautifully highlighting where you have been searching externally when the way to change your behaviour to the energy of what you seek is all internal.

Another example and a truth that is so present for many is being a single parent in a world where there is a lack of community. We were once fully supported by an entire village, now responsibility so often falls on the shoulders of one person alone. It is a lot to carry alone, and we have become so accustomed to just existing like this. When we find stillness to witness our response to our truth of internal and external happenings, we can find an opening to the next phase of healing. We find what is not in alignment to how we want to live and experience the world and we have the power within us to change it.

As a single parent, I found for so long that I wasn't able to drop into my truth of how exhausted I was. I had no idea because it wasn't safe to look yet. I had very little help around me and I felt if I collapsed, then how would I get the bills paid? How would I feed my children? I was the nurturer and the provider and I did it with little support and time for myself— so I, like so many others, stepped right into my masculine energy and very rarely allowed myself to soften, rest or to stop. After a long journey repairing my nervous system I discovered this way of life was not manageable or meant to be travelled alone, so I focused on building a support system around me. By the time my oldest son was sixteen I had taught myself to reach out for support, which was huge because I didn't know how to ask for help. I realised it wasn't too late to change it— I didn't have to keep doing it alone. I had to learn to soften into asking for help and commit to taking regular breaks without freaking out about how life would go on when I switched off. I had to embody a woman that invited ease into all facets of life. It was that or keep getting sick and burnt out, which kept the loop of the familiar sense of struggling going. It was like a struggle code was downloaded and I just decided to live by it and stuck to it like glue. I no longer chose that for myself and honestly part of me had no choice but to change it for health reasons. I was playing with fire this whole time but had no fuel left in the tank.

What is on the other side of your struggle has to be louder than the struggle loop itself, then know you can and will change it.

There are so many truths that can shift your perspective if you are willing to be with it. There are many truths being uncovered in the world today, but what is within us makes the biggest impact, and this is where we must start.

Start taking note of the truths within you that you don't mention out loud, or even question. Truths that show themselves in your body, behaviour or relationships and can filter into your life unconsciously, yet so very presently and consistently tapping you on the shoulder to take a look. Truth, although sometimes heavy and uncomfortable, can be a means to liberation. Some fear the truth, it leads to change and to the unknown. Some fear liberation from their own actual suffering, and I was one of them.

It is time to tune in and get comfortable with being uncomfortable so truth can rise. I know life can get confusing, and as much as the truth does set you free it can also bring discomfort and that's okay.

Wouldn't you rather be temporarily uncomfortable than hold on and create more suffering and dis-ease for yourself?

SUPPRESSION

To suppress something is to hide from it, to push it deep down where it gets stored within you, creating behaviours and beliefs that align with exactly what you are trying to escape. Suppressing something we find too painful to look at or be with, whether consciously or unconsciously, takes its toll. I've been down many of these suppressive rabbit holes out of sheer survival mode, which often happens when trauma responses are present. I didn't want to face a lot of things and the extent of my suppression only began to show itself when I was safe and supported enough to go into it. Prior to that I used alcohol and became a workaholic to keep the memories, anxiety and hardship at bay which meant I put myself in situations that were not aligned to my inner truth, but rather to the story I was hiding from. I guess if I thought I was having fun and pretending work never ended then I didn't have to look any deeper, and I certainly wasn't equipped with the tools in that time of pure fight or flight. I was far too busy holding it all together. It took me decades to even start to feel into my patterns of suppression and how long they had in fact been there, so you can rest assured it always comes at the right time and in the right way and you will know when. You will be guided there.

Suppression can be sneaky, especially when you have begun the self-development journey. I found myself keeping busy, creating distractions, telling myself I am in my purpose so it is okay to not rest or take a break. Even though I had moved past addictions and bad habits, I created new habits that in my eyes weren't so bad. But they still helped me dissociate and suppress. It was still too painful to actually feel how I lived my life for so long. I would get flashbacks to the time I left my marriage and got divorced when the domestic violence heightened. It was such an adjustment period for me to be out in the world on my own, I mean I had never been stalked before, I was in so much fear, and there was this other side of it where I also felt support for the first time in a long time. I now had friends in my kitchen cooking dinner when I got home from work, experiencing connection and care around me with beautiful loving people for the first time. I had never considered what I would do with free time in my very own house—there was a lot of newness around me so it was the subtle things I was catching myself doing when things felt hard that I would take note of. I was a damn good escape artist, the best I knew of and I have my children to thank for being the reason I kept grounded here through it all.

When I allowed myself to finally slow down or stop, I moved through periods of grief, and although this process took time and patience it was a beautifully surrendered acceptance of the past, allowing space to trust and open my heart towards life again, towards people. It felt heavy and joyful for me as I danced along the edges of what newness I felt was emerging. It wasn't until I slowed down that I realised the effect suppression still had on me. Creating circuit breakers in your habitual days is an amazing tool for transformation, to see what is there and if it is even yours.

When I spoke about domestic violence at a community centre's fundraising event, I was all in with my truth after coming so far, like guns blazing really. I was so willing to be vulnerable, figuring if I have a block about being judged then the only way through it is to do things that allow me to be judged. My shadow secretly loves going all in, being out of control and making sure if I'm doing it I am all in, sometimes at the cost of myself. And I am aware of how this hasn't always served me. I couldn't think of anything more terrifying than public speaking, especially about my own personal story, so naturally I went for it. Of course, the universe aligned me with an opportunity, and I got to tell my story for the first time in a room of about fifty strangers. Let me tell you it was indeed liberating but I crashed down hard the next day—I felt free but I also felt sad, vulnerable and cracked open, and it took me a few weeks to realise how big that experience I launched myself into actually was. From high as a kite on my own liberation to a bed ridden mess within twenty-four hours. I was too busy in the doing of it to notice or check in with myself, so focused on transcending the story that I didn't take the time to be real about how big it was for me emotionally and take the time I really needed to support myself in the process. The following weeks proved challenging, with swings into what felt like that black hole of darkness and fear swallowing me into the unknown. I suddenly dropped into the reality of what I had lived at a deeper level, separate from my story which I had never felt before because I always carried it. There was not so much anger anymore, but there was definitely a lot to process.

I lay in bed the days following the speech, just feeling it all. Thinking to myself, "Am I a thriver now?" I spoke of being a thriver out loud in front of all those people, so I wondered if I had come far enough to claim that. I had thoughts of, "Now they know things I haven't told anyone before and I can't hide anymore." The story was no longer mine to be personal with and I didn't know who I was exactly without it at first. I am now impersonal with my story because it does not define me. I don't think I had ever had a vulnerability hangover quite like that one.

After this process of realising busyness was a form of distraction for me, when I got real with that aspect of myself and slowed down enough to really feel it, things got super uncomfortable. They had to so I could release all the memories and stories that didn't align with me. I stood in it with an open heart, a fierce integrity and aligned in my authenticity. None of that shit I experienced is welcome in my life so being real allowed me to see how the sneaky things like keeping busy had replaced the alcohol I stopped drinking years prior to stop me from suppressing.

The adventure I embarked on with my own suppressive tendencies showed me how much I value aligned action and expansion, which for me involves self-care and slowing down. Embracing the realness of what I survived has brought a gentleness to my life. The key was in becoming still with it, without using suppression as a safer option, knowing we can regress and in doing so become even more gentle with self. When we realise we are finally safe, so much is then welcomed to the surface to clear, and although it can be messy it is also very beautiful, so if this is resonating please go slowly with yourself. You are not alone. Give yourself full permission to rest and repair while you do the work.

EXPRESSION OF AN ALIGNED SELF

You might be wondering what comes after seeing and knowing the truth that lives within us.

I believe the answer is to express oneself. We express our truth in writing, speaking, daily actions, releasing emotions, movement, creativity, and through the energy we share with the world. The choices we make when we know our inner truths are a direct answer to what we need to welcome in and embody, shifting what we know as we create the new way we show up in this world. We get the answers from within, and we ground them in the physical world via expression, allowing this embodiment to be a way to show up in our most authentic and unique essence. When we take conscious daily micro steps to embody our truth, our whole life changes.

You may find many ways of expressing your truth. Maybe you start to use your voice more to set boundaries that align with your values, expressing your feelings more, journalling to help expression move through you, or learning to ask for what you want more than you did before. You find a deep, connecting force inward when you take these steps toward accessing the truth and living it.

Expressing your aligned self doesn't mean you won't stuff it up from time to time. You will likely have to choose your truth again and again until it is a permanent way of being. It doesn't mean that the truth doesn't change for you, but it does mean you are conscious of what you create at a deeper level and you show up to it fully in each moment. By showing up in truth you will inspire everyone else to do the same and that is a very beautiful and much needed gift to others.

When you follow your intuition you will find it continues to develop. When you stop hiding and get out of your own way you will find that you were the only block. When you express your grief, you will eventually carry yourself in new ways, allowing yourself to live lighter. When you express emotions your body is healthier. It is not always easy healing through expression so it can feel very heavy, especially if you haven't been seen, heard or you hold secrets inside. Think of suppression like locking something away in a box that gets forgotten about, but really that thing that has been locked up is festering away in there. Sooner or later this box will be packaged up and sent straight to your front door. By the time you receive this package of your suppression it will show you it was not forgotten at all but rather now you may have a package to open and sort out that contains remnants of dis-ease in your body, unconscious behaviours that aren't serving you, patterns in relationships that aren't changing, more damage to repair in your career—or to your life. The impact of suppression always comes knocking eventually.

Now imagine expression being a key to that box (before it arrives to you as dis-ease in and throughout your precious life experience here.) Imagine letting it out little bits at a time so it can lighten the load carried and allow you to move forward in the way of truth, with acceptance and freedom. Knowing so deeply as you express yourself that you are not your trauma, you can be childlike again and play joyfully, making choices that serve you as a person that liberated themselves by choice and understanding. Then you have this experience of dealing with emotions, feelings, beliefs, and situations as they come. Take a moment to sense how beneficial this is for you, not to mention how healing it is for generations to come because *you* broke the cycle of suppression, because you used your voice, you were brave enough to choose your thoughts over someone else's, you got help, you enquired to your truth or even that you learnt to set those boundaries. This is how we make the change—it starts small and ripples out into your life via the embodiment of owning your individual truth.

LIVING REAL

When you come from an authentic place people all around you feel it. Once you become real with any expectations you have of the world or how it's been for you, the baggage you have been lugging around can lift with each action you take and the burden can lighten. In Buddhism, it is said that desire and ignorance lie at the root of suffering. If you crave anything and have wants that can't be satisfied, then desiring or holding expectation can only bring about suffering. Being real removes so much of the mental chatter that blocks you from reaching your fullest potential. Once you are real about your values and beliefs you will see magic all around you.

There is no better feeling than being in alignment to self. I personally feel that the freedom experienced by aligning to truth is complete liberation. You no longer need to be anyone else but you. You no longer need to carry what isn't yours. You can stop financing your energy with trauma and things that you think created who you are, and actually step into who you choose by following the road map of integrity. All energy loaned out from a place when you were not in alignment will return by simply choosing to be real with yourself. This also brings you to the present moment where it is much easier to make a choice from an aligned self.

ALLOWING TIME FOR INTEGRATION

So frequently we tick off a list like we are doing the groceries when we are dealing with transformation of the self. It is big work; we often do the steps, tick it off and move to the next thing like it's all done or there is rush and emphasis on the end goal. We can get stuck in the energy of constantly seeking. But eventually we remember there are always many layers to this existence. What we really need to take in when we go deep within to connect to our self and start living a new way is some down time for the in between, time to feel it all and time to be, especially when there has been a big completion or time of change. We need to be able to integrate the experiences we encounter into a new timeline of existing and rest when we need to because releasing the old can be exhausting work. It can take up emotional capacity to be in the self-work fully. Similarly to at the end of a big workday we actually need to do something that brings us back to ourselves, so doing the work to rewire and change your life really needs time for integration.

To embody a new way forward you will need time to just be with your-self. Time to settle in and get comfortable with the implementing of your learnings and to be with your new way of thinking, feeling, and embodying however that looks for you as you press on, so it becomes a lasting, transformational change. This prevents the common trap of getting over one hurdle then jumping straight to the next one, leading all too often to complete breakdown and overwhelm where you are left wondering what the hell just happened and who even am I? I am speaking from personal experience, and from what I have seen when journeying with others through change. It is easy to be overwhelmed and that isn't the ideal place to land after deep soul work. I eventually understood after many crashes from lack of taking time and integration that it didn't serve my growth and expansion to rush to the next thing. Everything needs time. And there is no limit to how much time each integration period will be. It needs to be felt and followed through into a solid lasting creation.

An example of integration: Whether you have learnt to open to your heart's energy or not, you can be in a practice of softening your edges as you travel over, under and through the waves of practicing. Daily practice to embody that softening might include Yin Yoga, dancing, breathing, time to sleep and rest, revisiting the food you eat that nourishes you, taking self-care seriously by committing to blocking time out in your schedule and following through because you know it comes from what is aligned to your truth. So be with it. Each thing that shows up—whatever it is for you—be there fully. Let it take as long as it takes and give it room to breathe. Give yourself the space needed to breathe that new life in.

RESONANCE

What I love the most about truth is that once you experience your truth you can no longer unsee it. If you go against it, you feel it in every cell of your body. So once you have realised what you stand for, what values you hold dear to your heart, and take time to integrate this amazingness into your life you will begin to vibrate energetically at a different frequency. You live aligned, and in your congruent state of being you create more of what you resonate with because you radiate your knowing so deeply it shapes the outside world around you. It really is magic.

You cannot control what you resonate with. Once we figure this out, we enter a whole new way of living. Setting boundaries becomes easier because we know we just cannot live out of alignment anymore or we feel it in our body, and it shows up as a fighting of the flow when we do. And quite frankly that feeling sucks. We learn what it feels like by not following our truth, more often than not we push it to its edge as we are figuring it all out because it is in experiencing the polarity we decide what is aligned and what is not. You might unconsciously choose the old way because it is known and safe but deep down you can feel truth urging you to get the hell out. Have you ever gone back to that old relationship to find it still isn't for you and nothing changed but you jumped right back in there and did it anyway, and you have the moment of, "Shit, what have I done" or, "I knew this was going to happen." Your inner truth knows and the sooner you become your own road map and let your truth be your leader the sooner you follow your personal thread through life—on path, focused, in alignment and in your fullest potential.

You don't experience your highest potential and access your truth by doing nothing; you have to be curious and willing to show up for it. You need to be willing to allow people who are not in full alignment with you to fall away as you choose your absolute truth and prepare to be free to be all of who you are with no apology. You will begin to liberate yourself from everything that is old, outdated and not serving you. These steps are beyond powerful in anyone's life and gives permission for those around you to do the same. I believe if we all lived a little more truthful to what is in our heart we could change the world.

When you go all-in with alignment to awaken all parts of yourself, you will find love, your version of success, universal support and abundance beyond what you ever dreamed of. You will begin to realise all parts of you belong, and despite the often uncomfortable journey home, you get to create your story from each present moment.

When I reached the point of understanding that I create my story from the present moment I felt a wave of relief wash over me. I remember the exact moment—I was at a workshop called Five Steps To Unlocking Your Potential and there was a moment where I said to the mentor, "I am who I am because of all the things that I have experienced, without it I wouldn't be who I am today." She said back to me with a look of knowing that she was about to give me permission to feel relief , "If you are impersonal with your story it doesn't matter what's happened, the past is the past, what matters is who you choose to be in each present moment." And just like that, one single point in time I was ready to hear, feel and know my story no longer had a hold on me. Now I figure what the heck, if it is my choice I may as well make the most epic story for myself. You can too!

THRIVING IN TRUTH

Let's talk about your will to thrive now. Being a victim for me feels stuck, like I'm right in the front row of the experience—it is super uncomfortable, loud and dramatic. It took cultivated awareness to know I'm sitting there, absorbing, getting involved, and to remind myself I can actually walk out of the shit show that is so far in the past and to know that there was no need to keep occupying the seat in the first place. I most definitely had a belief I was stuck; lucky these beliefs can change.

Being a survivor for me feels like I am taking action. Past feeling in the experience but I am still carrying the burden of it so it is easy to dip in and out of victim because I am still labelling myself as the person who is surviving the abuse, the toxic behaviour, addiction, or whatever it may be. In a way I feel survivor is the learning place and a very potent space to stand firm in self-discovery.

Thriving for me is choosing to go past what you suffered and the hurts you have been left alone with. Leaving that front row seat is huge! When I was there it felt like I landed in an enormous falsity of freedom. I was out of an abusive relationship and thought that's all I had to do, that if I get out it is done. In reality that is when the real work began for me. After this false sense of freedom was recognised, the healing really began, the impact of trauma was realised, which isn't an easy stage at all. Thriving to me means that all I experienced was still there; the difficult conversations, the triggers and responses to trauma, the person doing the toxic thing can still be doing the toxic things, your children may be going to that environment and having to navigate those transitions while you try your best to hold it all together. Just because you are a survivor the road doesn't end there. You can thrive wholeheartedly within the chaos of the shitty storms that come your way by developing tools for resilience to the unwelcome guests and responses constantly knocking—you thrive despite them.

Eventually I realised the storm was the consistent thing for me, it kept knocking me over while I played in it so one day I changed my perspective. The storm was something so out of my control so I thought to myself, "Why don't I use this time to centre myself, settle into the eye of this long drawn out nightmare and let it just happen around me?" Which led me to a mantra I would repeat in times I felt my centre get shaky. I would repeat, "Chaos is the perfect time to ground." And I taught myself to stay in my centre. Thanks to my situation, I was given so many chances to choose the chaos or the calm so

I feel that practice of finding stillness within me allowed me to find what my truth was and invite my energy back in for life. I realised the power was mine to claim and that my life could be more peaceful one choice at a time.

You choose to thrive just as you chose to survive. You do it because you reach a point in the journey of peeling back enough of the layers to reveal a deeper connection to self-knowing, what you stand for, how you deserve to be treated, and how you show up in the world. You arrive here, able to sit with yourself in curiosity and compassionate enquiry, communicating truth and creating awareness that this is what you are about. And if that doesn't sit with someone then they can take a seat in someone else's life and you can be more than okay with that. You will thrive anyway.

Thriving is choosing present moment responses while you may be taking the victim seat momentarily by having a response. It is knowing our perception of feelings, and whether they belong in that moment with us or not—the truth helps to discern this in every moment we experience as a thriver. In fact, I have so joyfully discovered you can use your past for fuel to live lighter and love deeper. The scars we have are sacred to our journey. They remind us of our strength and courage, our willingness to be alive, and as we begin to access our pain as higher knowledge we can channel that inner power to make aligned actions and change belief systems.

It is moving from woundedness to wisdom because what you have experienced can now be seen as your initiation into the empowerment of your divine self. Your greatest struggles can truly become the gateway to you discovering your fullest expression of truth and light. Gift yourself permission to shine and thrive in truth of what was then and what is now.

THE PLACE WHERE BELIEFS AND ACTIONS LINE UP

There is a sweet spot within this universal dance where you experience flow state, a state that we have all felt to some degree. You feel that things are just working out when you arrive here. Naturally you feel good about being in flow state because you are in alignment, there is clarity, vitality, less worry and you will sense that you are guided by something much bigger than yourself. That feeling of trust will feel strengthened. For example, you may have had a hard conversation with someone and showed up fully for it and even though it was uncomfortable you feel total relief afterwards,

Now that I live by my values and honour them as non-negotiables in this life, I find I'm able to hold more expanded awareness to my actions, emotions, words and thoughts. I feel that in honouring what I value in day-to-day life I'm creating an upgraded belief system and new timeline to walk upon as I evolve. It is fresh and unique to me and when I take action towards my personal evolution it feels like integrity at its finest—it really lights me up. After so much hardship I know the dedication it takes and I am nothing short of grateful I created the deservingness to remain lit up.

It is part of the experience here to dip in and out of these flow states, as everything is always changing and moving. I feel what links me back to flow is the practice of stillness, and creating circuit breakers to zoom out. Circuit breakers for me are those times I take to shake up reality, to re-connect to self, to ask myself questions about where I'm at, what is working, what isn't and to use those answers and space to re-align myself. If I have become busy for example (which is the one I still catch myself in the most), it is where my energy output has reached capacity. It is where I haven't checked in with myself and I feel worn out, which leads to inner frustration, criticism of myself like I 'should' be able to do more because last week I did, or it was 'planned to get done by Wednesday', closely followed by some projected snappy exhausted comments towards my boys and possibly some introversion as I pull away from friends and support. If I don't catch it soon enough I'll start to feel down and that is when I know to sound the victim alarm.

It's limiting for me to think I am in service and that is that, I really need those circuit breakers in my life to check if what I'm doing is still working, if I have a heavier load than usual to evaluate what is going on and ask how I feel rather than being in a constant output. I have to create space, to remember to receive so the output can be greater because I want to do big things in this world, and not all things we are called to do are easy or happen fast. This is a marathon of learning then living and living then learning—layer by layer. When it comes to living in a flow state I am now less worried about the when and how. I am more focused on what I need to do towards my higher purpose, to hold my light and honour my needs in the moments that pass so frequently, to take care of myself for this mission I have accepted and embraced, what my truth is, what my heart speaks, and there is ease and grace in that. There is no force. Forcing and confusion are both great signals of needing some space or realignment time to adjust and feel.

The answers are subtle here and it calls for you to keep old patterns and beliefs in check and hold integrity at the deepest level of honesty towards yourself before acting. If the actions and beliefs don't line up for you then you may experience lack, struggle and lower vibrational frequencies such as doubt and fear in your energy field. Sometimes you can even feel it through sensations in your body like anxiety. Think of a time where you knew of something that you had to do but avoided it. You didn't align action to what you believed deep down was best for you, for example you may have consciously or unconsciously put someone else's needs before your own only to find afterwards you experienced guilt, shame or a feeling linked to the past that didn't feel good. That behaviour will keep you stuck.

It is up to you to be in tune with your truth and be aware of what you are creating so you can discern what needs adjusting when you come to these opportunities for change—shifting either your action or your belief to align you to your truth at each opportunity. This gives you direct access back to that unique flow with self.

At the start of this book I talked about patterns, programming, conditioning and stories. At this phase of your growth and awakening journey, when you visit what your true essence holds you can more clearly see what you need to take on board or work on, what you run away from, and how you suppress or numb yourself because it is all linked to avoiding your truth, therefore blocking and dimming your beautiful light.

When being in your light and in your flow, you will in turn experience abundance.

INNER WORK REFLECTIONS

- **Embodiment exercise** - Feel into or journal one belief you want to shift. Write about it as it is now and perhaps the impact it would have if it remained the same. Then feel into how it could look different and perhaps some things you could do to align some action towards this new belief and what it brings to your life. Get curious.
- Shifting perspective can start with asking yourself right now—who are you without holding on? Exploring what that feels like for you can begin to open doors. Contemplate the sensation of holding on and see what cords are plugged into your energy that you could unplug from. Keep it simple and clear that space consciously with some nice deep breaths.
- **Circuit breakers** are a great way to come back to self, especially when we are in a spin. Create a really easy circuit breaker and write it down so you remember, one that you can practice next time you feel in a funk or needing a new perspective. E.g.- It could be having a song handy to dance to after you have had a bad day, or knowing you need to feel emotions so sitting in those emotions but having your joggers at the front door to walk around the block when you are done, or a yoga mat

on the floor ready for you to move or breathe when this time calls for it. These circuit breakers will support your integration processes and help energy move through you when it needs to.

- **Mantra.** Find a statement that resonates with you to repeat and work with over time. It will be unique to you. E.g.- I was so shocked when my life started to become less of a struggle so to curb those negative thoughts of, "This is not going to last" I created a statement of, "This is the new way for me." I would notice the negative thought, know that it had its place to be there then I would think, say or write, "This is the new way for me." It helped me to embody a sense of ease after so much struggle. So find your statement and get familiar with it. Let it get familiar with you.

Embodiment of Ease & Freedom

Looking through an unlimited lens
Possibilities flow infinitely into all of life
Entering new timelines with ease
And it's fast if you're willing
Deserving of all love that comes through
Being unconditional with self
Joy, play, and being seen arise
From within then all around
Chosen in entirety
Wholehearted living
Enjoying each moment
Truth aligned
Embracing power
Success in own eyes
Free being choosing, Love
Acknowledging the path that's before you
Acknowledging you can also flip the script
Create something new
Action the change
Choose words wisely
Choose thoughts humbly
Don't wait to believe.

- Jessie Moss -

8

Inner world awakening

> STOP ACTING SO SMALL, YOU ARE THE UNIVERSE IN ECSTATIC MOTION
> - RUMI

CHALLENGING AND CHANGING BELIEF SYSTEMS

In a world of outdated stories and inherited unconscious behaviours, be one who doesn't lose yourself. One to love who you are. One that doesn't need validation because you deeply know you are whole already exactly as you are. Learn as best you can to recognise the accumulated falsities in your program that do not belong to you.

Be willing to learn a new way forward. Be willing to move toward change. Be one to choose the path for yourself and lean into supporting yourself by finding the answers you seek within. Be one who continues to ask questions to all the parts of you, so you begin to change the story and keep centred in a world designed for following.

And if all else fails...

Just be.

IN THE VOID OF TRANSITION

There is a time when we arrive in the void of transition, where it can feel like nothing is happening or too much is happening. We can even feel stuck or like we are going backwards. The good news is this is normal, albeit frustrating or uncomfortable. The journey is to accept you are in the transition to change rather than resist it, which can be easier said than done. This, like everything else, takes practice and awareness. It is important to be kind to yourself when moving through times like this as the ego is moving through a death and you enter a rebirth stage as you evolve. I felt it was important to purely mention that this is a very real thing, and it is okay to be here.

If you could imagine standing on the edge of the unknown looking out at endless opportunities you once blocked for yourself because a part of you was limited, and now it is here for you because you moved through an experience or choice that has allowed you to be open to it. You are on the edge of change at this point. Imagine your entire known world up until now is what you are standing on. It is behind you, safe, and comfortable in a sense. Most of us feel this edge and don't explore past it because there can be so much fear.

Transition brings you to this edge of unknown again and again to choose. Will you stay in the known or will you see what is in the next stage of evolution for yourself? It takes faith over fear. Faith asks us to believe in divinity, that it is all as it should be. Having faith and trust in universal Source, God, or whatever you prefer to call it. Once faith replaces the fear on any edge you stand on you will take the next step. Whether you are aware of it or not, you may have moved through many of these transitions already, experiencing opportunities you never dreamed of on the other side of change.

Maybe it was a relationship breakdown that was the saddest time of your life, but it made space for you to eventually connect with a love you never imagined was possible. There are many chances for change and this is my point; allow yourself to be in transition knowing everything changes, so to have faith in your process is the invitation of grace. Next time you come to a choice of leaning into change or avoiding it, ask what faith would do over fear and really give yourself that chance to explore your faith.

I once dreamt of working my own hours from home, with flexibility, and being with my children every afternoon because I felt I had missed so much with them, but I never fully took the leap of faith because I was the sole provider, and a single parent with responsibility damn it, so I believed I was not allowed to create space for fun and play and that programming for me came before any dream I had. I had to cross bridges of fear, judgement, releasing the struggle mentality I so tightly held onto, and I want to mention learning to receive was also a huge part of this process.

Eventually I changed my work to walk this path in energetics. I built a new client base, lost a lot of clients, and some people thought I went woo woo crazy and either outwardly judged me or stopped talking to me, but I stepped into my purpose so it didn't matter to me once I arrived there. I invested in myself and hired a coach even though I had no idea how I was going to afford it, but I really felt I had nothing to lose at this point—I had already lost so much and rebuilt myself time and time again—this was no different. I realised the value I held in expansion and how I was the only one in my own way so I started to speak my truth more, I became a writer and I even learnt how to surf while the kids were at school. I landed smack bang in the middle of my dream of working from home so I could be with my sons in the afternoons. After practice and a whole lot of trust I started working smarter not harder.

Even though this whole experience felt hard and terrifying I did it anyway. I felt a time for living in ease was on the way and I craved it so badly that I started to believe I deserved it! I struggled my whole life and there I was, thirty-five years old and still creating the same old story. Then it hit me. I was also teaching my boys to struggle. I would repeat to myself, "I have it all" and felt deeply there was so much rightness to this whole transition. I pinch myself not only at what I created then, but how I allow myself to chase and create even bigger dreams now. When I landed on the other side of this transition I instantly wondered, "What else is possible?"

Transitioning is a space I work in often. What I generally tend to witness is six main phases so I want to break these down for you to provide clarity.

STAGES OF TRANSITION

STAGE 1 - Falling Apart - This is the breakdown so you can rebuild. In this phase we usually get all grippy and try our best to hold on to the old because the unknown is scary.

STAGE 2 - Entering the Void - This is when you realise you actually want something different, and part of this process is recognising you are choosing different even if you don't know what it is. You can feel quite lost and uncomfortable here.

STAGE 3 - The Void of Transition - This is where you do the work, you gather information, you realise there is a hurdle in the form of a block, and you work towards clearing it. Still feeling quite uncomfortable with some empowered bursts of 'I got this' from time to time.

STAGE 4 - Rebirthing - A part of the process where you hold the willingness to change. You start emerging and seeing more clearly what is on the other side of this transition.

STAGE 5 - Embodying - With clarity here you begin daily practices, choosing in moments you know have arrived for you to choose differently and take those practical steps to being in a new way of existing now.

STAGE 6 - Transcendence - Out of transition, through the practices and feeling steady, grounded in the embodied lesson of what you were transitioning through. Enter celebration vibes... until the next layer of the onion appears and you return to step one.

It is helpful to be with the energy of your transition, to observe it from a higher perspective, let the universe sort it out and know when you need to make a move and when you need to stay. Let life happen for you, not to you.

INNER WORLD WISDOM

The external world shapes us in early life because of the tribal roots, or sense of belonging to tribe, how we relate to each other and what we learn and absorb as we are growing. There comes a time when everyone, whether they choose it or not, connects to their own self-identity away from tribe, and in turn finds connection to their own heart. This heart journey inspires connection to nature, people, universe, self, animals, and it is a different way of being in the world especially if there has been a heavy reliance on tribal mentality, or any kind of fear in stepping out on your own. To seek the inner sanctuary of your very own heart, you find a truth that is deeper than before. This is where courage isn't found in the external, it is now able to be found deep within you and it shows up as vulnerability. When there is expression of the self we automatically access our own innate wisdom, discovering the answers were inside all along. When we stop looking outside of ourselves we turn inward—this is your inner world where you are past knowing and in wisdom.

The inner world is where intuition lives, like a navigational system we were born with but one we must find and reconnect with if we have forgotten this gift. We sadly aren't taught to access and harness intuition at school, along with many other important life skills and ancient healing methods such as breathing and meditation—such simple practices that could create so much wellness in the world and alleviate so much suffering. It is therefore up to you to find your intuition, which takes practice. How many times have you just known something but doubted the message, only to see it show up again perhaps a little louder, until it actually unfolds the way you sensed, confirming you knew deep down all along. This is intuition.

DEVELOPING INTUITION

Intuition is instinctive, it is an already known sense and it isn't to be reasoned with. It just is.

For example, from the work I have done as an intuitive, for me it meant that I first had to feel safe to be in a space of accessing my gifts (and we all have intuitive gifts.) My fear of judgement was blocking me from tuning in, plus I was very disconnected to myself during my time of victimhood and surviving, which was a large portion of my life allowing myself to be controlled rather than led by self. So, if you are feeling disconnected then take steps to connect to your inner world, creating awareness to it. That is the first point of action.

After connection, which can be via meditation, finding stillness, breathing consciously, noticing your dreams, being in nature, yoga or other spiritual practices of going inward, you develop an acceptance of your wisdom. The more you visit the inner world the clearer things will appear in your life externally. Trusting in your wisdom gets to be a practice and a deeper process in following your thread in this life, where you experience that flow state more often, and where you experience profound synchronicities, insights and connection to oneness.

Connect inward and trust, with no agenda other than to be still, and you will notice everything changes moment to moment. There is no rule book to how your journey is meant to unfold to the inner realms, but you will feel subtle messages and energies when you are open and willing to receive them, without forcing anything. Be still, go in with your breath, create space from the external world and your identity there, and see what you find. Be led purely by your instinct to access this gift of the present moment. The more you listen and take action to create times of stillness in that sacred place within you the less you live in the past and the less you worry about what is in the future.

Presence calls you.

GOING INTO THE SANCTUARY OF STILLNESS

You may begin seeing the external world and the inner world as different places, experimenting and getting curious with how you want your external world to feel and to shift to a place of working on it from the inner world.

What is inside you right now that is shaping what is going on around you?

Do you perhaps hold unworthiness within that creates abandonment on the outside?

Can you be aware of any mirrors being held up in the external world asking you to look from within? It is all a reflection, so to turn to the inner world is a powerful step and this is where I work with my clients and see the biggest shifts—always.

In the sanctuary of those moments of stillness where things either make sense or they don't, what is most importantly felt is that everything is impermanent, everything is ever changing, and you cannot cling to things no matter how hard you try, whether it be a relationship, a job, or your identity. Change is inevitable, which is great news because once we take control of what is happening within us we get to shape the world around us.

If I were to work with my clients from their external world only, I feel like we would constantly be focusing on what is outside of their control and choice rather than what they have power to choose in the moment from the place within them that is still and presently aware of their truth. Some people just like to have control and be in control of everything, let's not deny that. Sometimes control pushes people away and creates resentment within. To keep pointing fingers, giving tasks to people, having to have everything the way you want it is exhausting and it can also keep the problems outside yourself rather than seeing the problems or shadows within—choosing the path of control makes for one hell of a very long road to healing.

Imagine waiting for what could feel like forever for an external factor to change to make everything better and magically you didn't have to look at the shadow self—you could be seriously clinging to some distant hope it will be different instead of being with the truth of where you are right now, knowing that it's okay to feel the way you feel. The truth is, all we can control is what is within us. No one has control over what happens in the external world—it is an illusion. Take a seat in the fires of change and know you can do the hard things, let control loosen its grip on you (and everyone around you) and choose to see and make friends with those shadows. There is both light and dark within us all and there is always the practice of balance present.

When I get to know the external world of a client, I get an idea of what is showing up for them and shaping them from what they are choosing. But I always take them to the inner world to do the work. The external world holds information, and sometimes there actually are external things to work on like safety, survival, practical tools to leave relationships or jobs, how to communicate better in the external world when setting boundaries. Physical issues arise here too.

But when we move from the information gathered from the external world to working from the vast expansive spaces of the inner world, whether it be issues of money, sex, relationships, illnesses, you name it—when we find the root cause of what is internally going on then the external world shifts for them. They access their inner knowing, they come to feel a sense of relief and rightness and that their path, even if it felt painful, was in fact a gift to the moment they are experiencing when they discover the inner world's wisdom.

I cannot stress this enough—go within. If you don't like your job, friends, relationship, or life then go in and feel into your why. Then see if you can start asking questions to the highest part of self and feel crazy enough to have those questions answered. Become self led not story led.

If you feel something deeper calling you like you are not living in purpose, go in. That is where the answers always are. Go in. There is usually a time during this stage of stillness and self-inquiry that calls us to be alone when we first embark on this deeper soul discovery. It is a good idea to honour that time alone if possible, away from distractions to rest, repair and develop that connection to your inner spiritual sanctuary. It is simple here. We don't need distractions. We may find friends change, relationships change, the external world as we know it changes—be brave as you enter the inner realms of you and remember from this place that everything—absolutely everything changes and if you let the inner world guide you, what you once knew to be a way of life can be experienced with so much more depth, joy and sense of purpose.

Nothing is permanent.

FOLLOWING THE THREAD

From the inner spaces of you imagine there is a thread that is leading you down the path of truth. It is your experiential truth, which you can feel becoming more prominent in life the more you tune into it, and it just feels right. It doesn't always give you practical, specific directions but it does guide you ever so subtly. By focusing on your vision within the inner world and paying attention to what is there, we no longer drift from ourselves (or as far from ourselves) and we no longer indulge or plug ourselves into old energy.

By focusing on that connection to self you invite new energy into your life in every moment. Sure, it is easy to get distracted by temporary pleasures that once got you through being in that older energy, but you soon realise you don't live there anymore, and the temporary benefit is no longer serving you. For example, you might find you no longer desire to drink alcohol because there is nothing to suppress, or you no longer need to ask everyone else for advice because you have faith in your own internal navigational system that guides you so beautifully. You no longer focus on the negative or things you dislike, but rather hold compassion in relation to what once felt like an aversion for you. You will experience more peace on a daily basis.

There will be more depth infiltrating your life too. There is understanding that the mind will want to go back to the known because it is comfortable, familiar and it may not know another way just yet, and that's okay. You will go within perhaps a little quicker each time and begin to discern what is for you with more certainty and ease. This is how you stay in alignment with your highest self. The feeling of your vision and path will become so vital that the old will become quiet, you will travel less frequently to the past (or future for that matter), which brings more awareness in the present. This is what we can cultivate inside of us, within our system of innate wisdom waiting to hold and support us no matter what shows up. There is a lot of strength found by going in, it is where you build that resilience and faith muscle so you can follow that thread to your best life.

DISCERNMENT

Moving through the process of shedding your past over and over really begins to highlight what your experiences have shown up to teach you. These are your lessons and learnings. Your past doesn't define you in the present moment which is important to remember, that's why it is essential to establish commitment to self and to spend time going inward, to notice the breath and to access that inner peace. This leads to discernment of truth and right choices for you. And I am talking about your truth, not other people's truth, or the tribal truth to which you were raised on, I'm talking the highest truth to what you experience moment to moment.

Buddha teaches:

> Believe nothing, no matter where you read it or who said it, unless it agrees with your own reason and your own common sense.

CLARITY IN PERCEPTION

Your perception of reality when clear is your ticket to being in flow with everything around you. Everything is energy making up matter and mind. This reality is in constant ebb and flow, and I believe we only experience feelings of being stuck when we forget our truest nature. We forget because this world isn't designed for us to remember yet, that is why we are still constantly evolving. When we practice staying plugged into the wisdom of knowing nothing is actually staying still for us, that even our own matter (body) is constantly shifting and changing moment to moment, we can then have the clearest view on all we experience unfolding before our very eyes, exactly as it is.

I really like to hike mountains when I need a shift in how I am viewing myself or situations I am experiencing. One day as I sat on the top of this beautiful mountain, it was springtime in Australia so the warm morning sun hit my face as I reached for my water and took a seat near the edge where I could lean on a tree. I could see an eagle flying so effortlessly, and I was viewing this from above rather than below. I usually look up in admiration of an eagle gracing the sky.

I could see a clear view of everything below—the ocean, the town and houses looking tiny—and this beautiful bird, representing freedom in every soaring movement. I watched with such delight and awe. To be on top of that mountain was a physical example for me. I was grateful for zooming out of what I normally see and changing perspective. Usually the houses seem so big when you are standing in the street looking at them. Rather than being in life happening to me or for me, I was looking at everything from a spacious perspective where small problems seemed not so bad, where I could check my perception of reality as it truly was with space to think and feel and then to let be as I gazed at the undeniable beauty below.

The mountains remind me to practice this in moments where clearer perspective is calling. It doesn't have to be a mountain that gives you the reminder, it can be one intentional breath, dropping into a meditation to expand or a choice to just take a moment and re-centre yourself. I was reminded on this particular day that I can take a break, everything keeps moving without me, that it felt important to me on how I returned to life after the rest and how I responded to what the rest taught me that is in my absolute power. When my perspective is clear and aligned I know all is well, I know I will be making those aligned choices to my wisdom, compassion, values, to how it is important for me to show up in this world from a clear space.

Ignorance to the true nature of this reality we are experiencing right now will only have you identifying with the struggle within yourself. There are things that we label out of ignorance, things that feel good and you want more of, things that feel bad so you want to get rid of them. The choice we make from our perception can make things seem easy or hard, creating ease or causing resistance. All labels from easy to hard and all that is in between, have you choosing how you view your life through your perception of reality.

Your experience is happening right now, so with a calm mind, and with acceptance of all that is, cultivating positive from negative, maybe even eventually knowing nothing is good or bad you can begin to free yourself from suffering.

Everything just is.

SUPPORT

There is a momentary forgetting of support when I feel everything has fallen apart for me, only to see the foundation was stripped away and rebuilt into pure magic. I smile. Touché Universe. I spill endless faith into Source as it has always been one solid & consistent resource for me. It has my back and whether you feel like it or not, it's got yours too. I know I have felt lack of support cripple me at times, I have felt the depth of loneliness and the shame of being different. I raised two boys mostly all by myself, away from my family, outside of any support systems and through the traumatic experiences I wasn't always sure I would make it through.

Being a mum at the age of nineteen I don't feel I have been alone in the physical world, my feelings of loneliness went much deeper than that. There have been many points in my life I ran from my trauma and triggers, I did a lot of moving and re-establishing some kind of life I could with the little energy, faith and hope I had left for myself at the time. Over and over, throughout my whole life, running, moving, only to find my problems were following me—I couldn't even drink them away although I gave it a good go.

Sometimes Source was all I had when I hit rock bottom, so I don't write about support lightly. Those moments where I wanted to give up, where I was harassed so badly I would think of handing my son over just to alleviate the pain and suffering I was living for so long, I was a shell of what looked like a functioning human. I felt dead in those moments, and scared so when I urge you to lean into the support of your inner world know that there is nothing fluffy or wishy washy about that connection to the divine I speak of.

Sometimes we have no choice but to lean into ourselves and experience this support from within if we want to make it through. I know when I first really felt this universal support it was through the depths of sheer terror and pain. I found myself praying at times for help, to take the pain away, to make the awful external things stop, to keep me safe when I was followed, watched, receiving death threats and my house was broken into.

I found connection to the divine workings of spirit alone, desperate, crying on the floor, with nothing to my name, drunk. I found it when my youngest child was three and he was taken from day care—I didn't know where he was and how I would get him back. Through all my troubles, external storms, through my joy, empowerment and liberation I keep this connection close now. And like anything the more we practice this the easier it gets.

If you feel a lack in support, love, or anything right now... see if you can feel support from the elements, from source itself. Experience it for yourself. I want you to know today and all days the place of sweet stillness and unlimited support is available and willing to be there for you too.

How much are you willing to feel it?

INNER WORK REFLECTION:
MAPPING YOUR FOCUS INWARD

Draw yourself or a shape that represents you on a piece of paper. Then draw a circle around it leaving enough room to write all the things that are in your power to choose. Then outside of that circle begin to list all the things that are not in your control. This will give you an instant visual of what you can bring your focus to, especially those times you experience struggle.

Things inside your bubble that you can focus on are things like your responses, your daily practices, the way you speak to people, and your personal choices etc. Things that land outside of your bubble (things you can't control) may be things like how another person decides to treat you, the weather, what kind of customers show up at work or whether people listen to you.

Remembering this simple exercise allows you to see what resides internally and externally. The more we shift our focus towards what we do have choice over, what place we speak and live from, what our truth is, then we no longer tend to get caught up externally trying to control other people, situations, or focusing on what is uncontrollable and scary. We realise what is in our control and by turning in we work from a focused space on commitment to self, really flexing that muscle of showing up for ourselves in these moments. It is knowing the difference between your inner world, your sanctuary of peace and your external world, the world happening out there, outside of you.

A Meeting with alignment

Found values by trial and error
No straying or taking a dive for
what cannot meet in a field of integrity
Like the sun
worthiness shines out of eyes
opened by rejection and choice
Heart swells joy from inside out
Whole and humble journey
Absorbing it into thirsty cells
Seeking refuge in an all-encompassing uncertainty
Comforted in knowing there is but now
Now is all there is
A voice can shake and still rise
to a timely occasion of terrifying opportunity
In the name of growing an expansive soul
Arriving to divinity untouched yet so felt
One heart taking up resonance in all hearts
Uniquely on path and on purpose
In action align
In stillness receive
In this split-second retrospection
Remember a forgotten self
In awe of every in breath
Timeless moments to moment

OPEN

Moving, drifting, finding freedom in togetherness
Sweet wandering landscape changing
Shedding all the who am I
Becoming again
Always becoming
Come in
Stay a little longer
Align a little deeper
No need for words here

- Jessie Moss -

9

Gratitude in oneness

> LET'S TRADE IN ALL OUR JUDGING FOR APPRECIATING. LET'S LAY DOWN OUR RIGHTEOUSNESS AND JUST BE TOGETHER.
> - RAM DASS

DIVINE TIMING

Everything is as it should be. To truly believe this sentence in every moment can feel like hard work. Sometimes things don't feel like they are working out at all, and you can kick and scream about it all the way to some kind of breaking point or place where you reach the threshold of holding on. There you can let go of the grip on it in surrender, and this is exactly where the magic happens—in the letting go of any and all expectations.

Letting go looks like laying down any controlling tendencies or expectations to have something arrive a certain way, in perhaps a perfect sequence we have conjured up in our minds, or by a certain time. We can get so caught up in the vision of what it looks like and how it is coming. We can be so goal-focused that we may in fact create more obstacles to move through in the process—this stage I believe lives mostly within the mind, and we can't feel there. What if it was as simple as feeling it like it was already here? As if you were already sensing feelings of it here now, so your mind and body start to create this connection of logic and emotion to then drop in to truly feel it. By sensing the thing you desire here now, without needing to know the who, why, how, when, and what it looks like, by using your beautiful mind to imagine and really feel it as if it were already here—and then giving it gratitude—you can then release the stress that comes with logistics. What if it comes in quicker this way? Gratitude is the vibration of it already being here.

If you have felt it here now, then you have already invited the vibration into your experience. The next part of the process is to let it be and to trust so it actually comes in how it needs to. It sounds so much easier this way, doesn't it? It feels like less work and less trying really, but in reality I believe the practice of it can at first be a little difficult to feel into. This is because you are releasing control around having to know the details. You are simply just learning to feel it and then handing it over. Are you willing to land into that trust rather than pushing, trying to force it to fit your vision, being busy doing things to create it and getting impatient? Are you willing to see the behaviours you implement around manifestation that can stem from losing sight of the gratitude piece? Quite frankly it gets exhausting to work so much for things and it takes you back to the sometimes kicking, screaming, and controlling it to be a certain way part. When there is control present it might be a time to ask, "What am I afraid of?" Or "If I wasn't afraid what would I do?"

Fear of receiving what we ask for and desire sometimes is a thing. Gratitude allows things to grow. What do you hold, feel, and sense gratitude toward?

Can you see how it is creating more of those things, experiences or feelings in your life?

In my experience the more I try and force things to happen the more I seem to be learning from it. It once was a very cyclic pattern for me to work so hard so I could feel I deserved the goal at the end, or the pay check at the end of the week and I always only earnt just enough. I never got to the goal I dreamed of by working harder. I can say from full experience now that I arrived by landing in my worthiness of living a better life, by releasing the way I was working (the way I thought I had to work) to trust myself in making the right choices and knowing my value and gifts more intimately. The good news is we can change patterns. The more I simply feel it, give my life gratitude and hand over how it's going to work out for me, with faith and trust everything is as it should be, the more in fact works out for me and the more I can feel when it's time to take action.

I am not talking about this in a spiritually toxic way either where I just hand it all over and use the right words to make it all sound believable—this has to be felt, lived and part of your daily practice and commitment to self. Don't take my word for it either, try this out for yourself. And know that it is all perfect as it is, no matter how hard it feels sometimes. Everything in this moment is as it should be. It's how you've made it. It is gratitude that shifts our state and opens the doors.

FORGOTTEN ONENESS

Right now, we are traveling through a time that we will look back on in history and be amazed by. We have never been in a time quite like this before. I believe because things are changing so rapidly, we aren't taking time to slow down enough to even notice how much is trying to align you to a new way of being. A lot of fear and resistance is surfacing because it is a time of change and mass awakening on our planet. Many of us have stopped wondering.

We simply don't seem to remember everything is connected and that we have a choice. We have been conditioned to follow and most still do because there is an undercurrent of fear throughout the collective. When occupying a state of fear internally we are easier to control in the external world. The longer we stay in fear the more we spiral down into lower vibrational energies. When we forget that we are in fact one with all things, and that we are actually made up of energy, things tend to get very complicated for us. We forget to enquire about our true nature, the truest nature of us.

Let's expand our awareness. Let's bring the world to a higher frequency together by being more present with every choice, more connected to each other and nature, living with intention, integrity, and conveying consciousness through our actions, because it may well be our only chance at really making a difference in this experience.

TRAVEL WELL

Rather than constantly arriving and searching we begin to learn how to travel well, to enjoy each piece of the puzzle as it comes together with awe and wonder. We remember that each step on the journey to liberating the self is in each very moment and choice, not upon arrival—nor should there be emphasis on the arrival. To travel well is to be in all of it, as it is. To not miss a step on the journey and to count each one as a blessing.

After a long time searching, growing, learning, expanding and always leaping so far forward I was constantly landing right into this anxious overwhelm. Once I developed a profound trust within myself to know when to do the work and when to rest, I began to slow things down. In the slowing down I could see more, my gifts started to bloom and I realised I didn't need to be leaping. I could be in each step, giving myself permission to be in and not rush my healing. I found more clarity, too. For example, knowing I was scared of judgement, I allowed myself to feel the resistance to showing my true weird and wonderful self to the world, but I practiced doing things that felt scary to me. I started small, one step at a time. Things like public speaking, or changing my business to purely support people in their time of awakening and change. When I became more present with my why each step of the way it started to feel less scary. The fear in me eventually felt more supported and when my fear felt supported I knew I could walk through what was calling me with the fear present. I was showing my fear it was okay to take the action and that we were in it together.

The ability I discovered within me to discern what the absolute truth was for me eventually became clearer and clearer. The more I experienced what it was like not following or speaking my truth the more I noticed alignment all around me. A good example is dating. I learned a lot from dating, when someone wasn't feeling right the energy never lied. Once I was tuned in, when I felt something was out of alignment I learned to call it out with compassion, and I got to practice showing up as me with boundaries, hiding nothing. I have at times in my past tried continuing along a path that wasn't completely feeling right, but despite what I was feeling, I would be busy finding the good in everyone, ignoring the sinking feeling in the pit of my stomach which sometimes turned into a feeling of anxiety. If the sinking feeling had a voice I'm sure it would have said, "You know this is no good for you. You feel it don't you? It doesn't feel good ignoring the truth, does it?" And, "Have a look at your story of unworthiness just spilling out all over this." The voice would have said choose again.

I developed trust for my body, the messages it was giving me, and I sat with compassion as I enquired, to make choices in alignment to my values. It became a chance to show up more and more as myself, to speak my truth to others, and there was more rightness in that than continuing or entertaining something I knew was not for me.

It was through the process of being incongruent that I learnt what being in alignment to self really meant. It would be like me trying to continue a relationship with someone who wants to let's say, go to church, tame or shape me, and have three extra children straight after we buy a big old house where I would be stuck in domestication, while my passions for awakening and truth seep out slowly along with my life force energy as he tells me that's it—this is our dream and we made it! And while that is a beautiful dream for some, others may connect more to their spirituality with a Sunday surf and meditation, kids may never be on the cards, you may have a free spirit that cringed at what I just wrote and your truth may simply be you want to spend money on travel or you would be happiest living in a tepee. The truth is this person is not for you, albeit possibly incredibly amazing in other aspects of what relating with this person could offer, it may feel invitingly safe and what you maybe thought you needed (or what your parents hoped for you.)

My point is that you are going to reach your truth eventually so why wait until it's time for your last breath to hold even an ounce of regret that you got the big house, had all the kids, and stopped surfing because your programming and conditioning ran the show and you lived life making choices to serve other people's happiness rather than your own?

There was no rule book to finding my truth externally and there isn't one for yours out there either, it is within us. It must be remembered. I know for me it was far from anything I had ever been shown directly in any aspect of my life. I didn't feel I had role models of people living or speaking their truth until I was an adult and when I experienced it, it was so terrifyingly beautiful to me. I felt like I came here to learn things the hard way, to stay in my suffering without any tools until I had no choice but to wake up. And when I eventually did, I could finally see that my dysfunctional life up to that very moment of awakening was in fact exactly as it needed to be. I had been so very unconscious at the wheel that was steering my life, so I knew to feel everything that had been was somehow what I needed to learn so I could choose again—to know that in the moment I am who I am and it changes all the time.

I have experienced parts of my ego dying and I have laughed at it. Other times it is dying and it's like a scary, fearful death experience, especially while working with plant medicine in Peru. It was the one thing that has shown me there is so much more than just me. I am but a speck in this existence and yet connected to all of it. I have the ability to access unlimited opportunities and possibilities and so do you, but we cannot stay in one state permanently. This includes a state of bliss, or pure insight and clarity with no suffering, and nor should we want to be walking this middle path. Everything has a beginning and an end, which is what I tell myself before any big work or ceremony that I do so I remember no matter how hard it might get, I will land on the other side of it, in an energy of completion and purification, lighter than I was before. I know and accept in my reality what comes will have a reason to be there.

Each time I reach a point in this existence where I feel change coming or the calling to evolve, I take the opportunity because I missed those chances so many times before. I am often alone in the physical sense now rather than gathering with a lot of people. I get to choose where my energy gets plugged into or out of.

I have discovered that taking circuit breakers from life is really important, especially while it feels there is a constant expansion all around me. Time to tune out so I can tune in. One thing I notice is that people, including myself, really struggle to allow those breaks because we are often programmed to push through, hold on, suppress or suffer through something as I mentioned previously. We cannot create a new way for ourselves by living out old inherited behaviour. These circuit breakers allow us to zoom out from life, changing the perspective and giving us needed space. To breathe. To choose. To change. To become. To bring to life the integration of learnings. To practice returning to our precious hearts.

It is easy to find a million excuses not to take time out, but there is magic that happens in the stillness between the busy. We receive so much from stillness.

I no longer want to miss the expansive pauses between thoughts or action. The transitions and void spaces that feel uncomfortable and rushed have a place; it all has a place. Choosing ease at every corner calls for complete acceptance of the hardness to exist too. To accept where you have walked, where you are at right now, holding the vision of where you are going, and to accept all that surrounds you.

I feel this state of oneness and acceptance of all things is where we can thrive despite all that has happened up until now. In those moments between actions, with enough space to choose what seeds are sown, and if they are sown with bitterness or love. You get to choose with awareness and integrity along a self-led life. To be here now.

To travel well.

COMMITMENT TO CONNECT

This is an invitation to enquire about your commitment right now within your current circumstances, exactly as they are. How is your commitment to the connection towards self, and the essence of oneness that all is connected?

If you could get yourself to a point where you feel highly motivated towards holding commitment to the remembrance of self, it is important to note the present moment is your ultimate guide through all that you face. That place to land within where you discover time and time again new depths of yourself and quite quickly upon returning you embrace just how extraordinary your life can be.

We lose commitment to self through patterns of sabotage, some so deeply ingrained they might feel like they will take a lifetime to release attachment to or feel so hard to find. Things can get so messy, because our mind gets so messy. We complicate commitment to connection and we forget to keep it simple.

Holding a strong commitment to self requires holding yourself accountable to get up in the morning and choose again, to remember you have that power, to hold gratitude in the pure appreciation of being here now no matter what is going on for you, to feel that you are alive, to feel your heart beating, to simply breathe.

However we experience it, we all know this place inside of us, even if it's been brief visits. We feel it when we are connected to our light, our spark, our dark, our mind, our body, something much bigger than matter. We came here with a sense of awe and wonder, yet maybe somehow the wonder of it wasn't enough for us to stay with fully and it got so damn complicated. You can choose to strip it all back to simplicity now or you can continue to live with lack of connection and commitment to your true self. We have times of wondering and times where we wonder more about ourselves and our own issues, which only amplifies them. We forget so easily what we came here for; to remember our divine selves and commit to the connection to it with awareness, allowing the most awe and wonder-filled experiences to touch us while we are here. To live fully. The trouble is we tend to believe that we have time, which leads to the world taking so much for granted.

THE END OR THE BEGINNING...
An invitation to remember

Take a nice deep breath in and out. Beginning to feel the self. Mind-Body connected and open.
Feeling into a centred place that resides, always, within.
Go in with the breath.
Connected to source, feeling connected to your own beautiful divinity.

Connected to the place that seeks the simplicity of the deepest truth of your very own heart. Focusing gently upon a higher spiritual perspective of your life path, knowing from here your prayers are always answered, you bring to your life what you create from these exact moments, in the perfect time it comes, in the perfect way it comes, which could be how you in fact least expect it to have come in at all.

Here you let go of it all. Just breathe it out, gently, stepping out of your own way ever so softly.

Here you already have everything you need, you are whole already, past the fear of the unknown, past the grasping and controlling, way past any doubts, start to soak in a profound confidence into your self. Breathe it in, soak in the gratitude, soak in the healing you have encountered up until now, revel in the uniqueness that is your path and where you are right now upon it, knowing the choice is yours, the choice to take sanctuary within your spiritual connection whenever you need to feel centred, it's all here always waiting for you to choose it.

No matter what is happening around you, embrace the journey of what it feels like to be you, in this very body.

Beautiful being, embrace your truth fully, and then live from there.

Know that it's all going to be okay. Know you are blessed with more wisdom than you may ever fully know, know that you are an unlimited being, you are light.

Know and feel that you are love.

INNER WORK REFLECTIONS

Contemplation of your beautiful life:

- What are you stepping into?
- What no longer serves you?
- Where could you be more curious within yourself?
- What is your focus on?

Write it out, talk it out, dream about it, meditate on it, bring it into your field in whatever way feels right and start to see how the inner world shapes your outer world.

It truly is a beautiful life. An inspiring, change-making time to be alive.

Asking us all to step intentionally onto a new timeline, a newer version of ourselves, if we can start doing this IMAGINE the opportunities and change we could see in this time of living.

If you are not feeling awake yet, it is most certainly time to wake up, rattle the cage and free your fine self into endless possibilities.

New Earth is already here.

As above So below

I earth I remember who I am
I soar I remember who I am
And into surreal dreamlands
Past ocean as deep as my soul
Into the black of the night sky to wisdom
Timeless wandering
Spacious edging unknown expansion
How free it feels to be here
How trapped the paradox
If I could show you one thing
It'd be how amazing your light is
If I could tell you one thing
It's that you are whole already
If I could help you feel one thing
It'd be expansive limitless infinite love
And then I'd give you the gift of remembering
Over and over again
So you could meet yourself fully
Knowing you are but a speck in existence
And the whole entire universe all in one. One.
We are one, connected. Earth, sky, soul, heart.
It's time we start remembering.

-Jessie Moss -

ABOUT JESSIE MOSS

Hello beautiful souls,
My name is Jessie.

The work I choose to do is invisible to most. It requires trust and willingness so if you have come this far in the book I want to let you know how much I respect the journey you have just been on. I am proud of you.

I tend to be found by others in the midst of change so I'm not a super fluffy, relaxing, all-love/light kinda facilitator.

I happily dance with the shadows too.

I believe when we create safety within and together while going to the more uncomfortable places, so much healing can take place as there are many gifts and answers lying dormant in there!

I will always believe all parts of you belong and you are whole as you are.

I don't follow a structured healing modality (that I know of).
I follow my intuition and right now mostly somatic-based psychic abilities to connect logic and feeling to ages, beliefs, and parts of the self which I feel allows people to experience their wholeness.

I thrive in truth and knowing we always have the choice to choose again. We can all do hard things, talk about the unspoken, and heal what we may think is unhealable.

The work I did on myself after I decided I was all in was at first to survive. Following that reason, I was so desperately seeking this "home" feeling, and now looking back I simply wanted to feel understood and like I made sense to people.

Now I am on a journey of piecing the puzzle together for others and in this beautiful experience of authenticity and awareness that always expands me beyond what I thought possible.

I really wanted to share a liberating and useful tool in book form.
So here we are...

I decided one morning that I would be a writer when the pandemic hit and there was no work to go to for a while - I had never written much besides in my journal but I found writing an easier way to express myself. This book is what happened--- it's taken me on a journey around, through, and into the power of words, intention, and my own heart. The words in this book were written to be felt.

ABOUT JESSIE MOSS

I'm a big believer that fear is a great opportunity to land on the other side of an edge, changed and a little more whole within.
Is this how we can change the world and let love lead?

So this is where I'm at.

You might wonder where I was before all of this.

From the age of 17 when I had my first acknowledged awakening I had no idea what was going on, why was everything so hard, who was i, why don't I fit in the school system, why are we here.. so many questions, followed by so much anger.

At 19, I wanted to work as a healer it was the only thing that made sense to me but I was too scared of judgment.
So first, I was a make-up artist and beauty therapist until the body began to fascinate me so deeply that I became a

massage therapist. Massage therapy was a great initiation into working with people in the physical sense but also learning just how important energetic boundaries were.

So I dove deeper into many different healing modalities, workshops, and books - lots of books.

Through my twenties, I couldn't study enough because I still had an active program running where I would seek validation externally so I also became a personal trainer and fitness instructor. This was the time I built strength in my body and my mind. I started to feel my lost self emerging and looking back it's where I found the inner strength needed to get out of my marriage and reclaim myself again.

All of a sudden one day it didn't seem to quite make sense that after years of trauma to keep exhausting my body, pushing myself so hard, and going that fast. It was temporary relief for my anxiety, PTSD, and stress responses so I began to look deeper.

Yoga was one thing that highlighted my anxiety at first, how helpful to learn that temporarily sitting in my emotions allowed them to process through me and I started to experience spaciousness, I started to feel calmer and I began to sleep therefore I started functioning like I hadn't in a very long time. I learned to rest so my nervous system recalibrated and I chose a new life one day at a time.

Feeling reborn I became a student and teacher of yoga, pilates & meditation. I now work one on one with clients, host events that incorporate sound healing and inner-world journeys and built an online course to merge all the practices that helped me into one place.

ABOUT JESSIE MOSS

I teach that we are not our stories, a remembering of choice and how to align to it from within.
All the paths I journey deep down have led me to heal and to teach healing from a place of vulnerability, and through dedication to heart-centered practices.
Always choosing to **open**.

I hold a knowing that my personal challenges toward experiencing growth and understanding are some of my greatest teachers. The chronic pain and injury helped me learn to trust the body knowing how capable of healing it really was, and I lived through times of hardness to learn I had a choice to rewire my belief systems and behavioral patterns if I wanted to change my reality.

All of the modalities I have studied along the way blended with life experience, the beautiful human and plant teachers that come and go have

ABOUT JESSIE MOSS

so divinely led me on the path to be here now. From there all I can do is work on myself and choose integrity. What happens from that alignment is always so magical.

This book was written for the highest good of all beings.

Many blessings,
Jessie

8 WEEK ONLINE JOURNEY THROUGH THE ENERGY CENTRES

Alignment to Awakening

Your vision will become clear only when you look into your heart.

Who looks outside, dreams.

Who looks inside, awakens.

Continue the journey...

Please receive a **33% discount** on this course as a gift from me to you by using the code **OPEN33**

Alignment to Awakening will give you the tools internally to shape the world around you from the inside out.

Find out more about the online course @ jessiemoss.com/shop/

THANK YOU

THANK YOU

THANK YOU

Connect

📷 jessiemoss_intuitive

▶ Jessie Moss - YouTube

f www.facebook.com/jess.moss.7

✉ awakening@jessiemoss.com

Printed in Australia
AUHW011811191122
371469AU00010B/9

9 780646 860527